A PATTERN OF WINGS

A PATTERN OF WINGS
and Other Wildfowling Tales

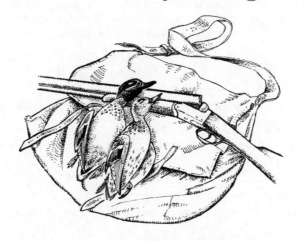

EDITED BY

Jonathan Young

Drawings by John Paley

UNWIN

HYMAN

LONDON SYDNEY WELLINGTON

First published in Great Britain by the Trade Division of Unwin Hyman
Limited, 1989.

Unwin Hyman Ltd
15/17 Broadwick Street, London W1V 1FP

Allen & Unwin Australia Pty Ltd
P.O.Box 764, 8 Napier Street, North Sydney, NSW 2060, Australia

Allen & Unwin NZ Ltd (in association with the Port Nicholson Press),
Compusales Building, 75 Ghuznee Street, Wellington, New Zealand

---

British Library Cataloguing in Publication Data

A Pattern of Wings : and other wildfowling tales.
1.   Great Britain. Wildfowlng
1.   799.2'44'0941

ISBN 0–04–440417–4

A compilation of post-war wildfowling stories must include those of the
wildfowling writers who contributed to *Shooting Times* in the 1940s
and 1950s. Their stories were masterpieces of the genre and so have
been included for the benefit of future generations. Sadly, however, it
has proved impossible to contact some writers' relatives, who are urged
to contact the publisher.

Designed by Caroline Archer
Set in 12/13 ITC Garamond
Printed by the Bath Press, Avon

To my wife Basia

CONTENTS

LIST OF PLATES

Plate 18 has appeared as a cover illustration for *Wildfowling – one winter's tale* by Alan Jarrett and is used by courtesy of Dickson Price Publishers Ltd.

INTRODUCTION

T HE FIRST frosts begin to bite in the northern countries. In the Baltic and Scandinavia the wildfowl become unsettled. Small trips of birds merge into ever-growing formations until the landscape's silence is rent by the swish of their companies and armies cutting the wind. Then, one day, they have gone.

The second week in October. A man crunches his way past the windfall bramleys down to his outhouse. A drake mallard, a slight red stain on its plumage, swings on its string to thump against the door as the man opens it. A hatful of field mushrooms is on the bench.

He takes down his waders and checks them for tears. He lifts his haversack off another nail, brushes it down and takes it inside. Watched by his labrador, he packs methodically, following the practice of his youth. (In those days he could never get to sleep before flight. He still finds it difficult.) In go the decoys, sandwiches, flask, compass and torch. He opens a cupboard, picks up his cartridge belt and splits open a box of heavy loads. Carefully he slides each one into a loop until only the brass protrudes. He leaves three empty loops in each end. Into these he shoves six goose loads. (Well, you never know.)

That night, the strong easterly intensifies, bringing with it the migratory wildfowl. Tomorrow the man and the wildfowl will meet again, eight months after their last appointment.

This book is about such meetings. It is not about the techniques or equipment of wildfowling, which are well covered by other books. Nor is it about shooting large bags of wildfowl, though some good bags are disclosed. Instead, it is about our love of wildfowl and wildfowling. This is a difficult concept for those who have not pursued the sport. How can we love wildfowl and yet seek their destruction? A friend summed it up well when he likened himself to a peregrine. For, unlike most people, wildfowlers do not study natural history. They are part of it.

The pure ornithologist, no matter how keen, can only be an observer. He is reliant upon his binoculars or telescope to bring him close to his quarry. Such optical equipment does not work well in poor light, for obvious reasons, and is susceptible to the salt and slime of the foreshore. And so he sticks to the sea-wall and daylight.

The wildfowler, in contrast, enters the food cycle. The moment he treads on the marsh he becomes the supreme predator, but only if his knowledge can put him within range of his quarry, a mere forty yards. How does he manage this? How does he ensure wildfowl choose his creek to flight over when they have miles of foreshore available? He achieves it by studying his wildfowl intensely. He knows when they flight and their flightlines. He knows their feeding habits. He knows their language and how to talk to them. He knows how to imitate their shapes. And in the final moments he knows how to listen to the whicker of their pinions, to recognize their silhouettes and flight patterns and how to shoot huddled up in a tight ball in a mud gutter.

The wildfowler loves his quarry for their sheer beauty: the chestnut of the wigeon, the glossy bottle-green head of the mallard, the teal's iridescent specula, the pintail's elegant form. And he loves the sky hound music of the wild geese skeins.

He loves the wildfowl for their environment. Man cannot interfere with the foreshore. There are no housing estates on the ooze. Those manmade structures that do exist are soon claimed, to rot, like the sailing barges, and be gradually encompassed into the marsh's grandeur.

It remains, then, a place of sea samphire and lavender, of fine turf and sand, where you can walk to flight in shoes, and of mud-filled gutters so sticky that fowlers have to tie their waders on. It is a place where mullet cruise in September and the phosphorescent sea larvae emit a shower of green light at every step. It is a place where good wildfowlers drown, men who knew the tides and winds intimately, only to have their calculations nonsensed by nature's vagaries. Who, then, can wonder that wildfowlers love their quarry?

The following tales reflect this love. Each is a true story. Some of them are reproduced by kind permission of *The Shooting Times*; others have been specifically commissioned.

The great post-war wildfowling writers are here, including Alan Savory, BB, Tower-Bird, Hugh Falkus, Michael Shephard, Petrel and Colin Willock, men who enjoyed the heady freedom of wildfowling in the fifties when much of the foreshore could be shot without hindrance and the quarry list was longer. Here too is a selection of the best of the new generation of modern fowling writers, including John Humphreys, Neoflak and Graham Downing, together with men like John Richards and Alan Jarrett who have devoted much of their lives to wildfowl and wildfowling.

Illustrating the tales are some of the finest living wildfowl painters – Geoffrey Campbell Black, Julian Novorol, John Paley, Ian Phipps and Jonathan Yule. Each of them a practical wildfowler, they display an awareness of their subject which has seldom, if ever, been bettered.

It is my great privilege to have been asked to gather all this talent into one volume. In so doing, I hope that others may share the excitement of what I consider to be the finest sport in the world. I have been very fortunate. Raised within gunshot of an estuary, I started fowling when I was thirteen and have subsequently shot over many of our great estuaries, as well as pursuing wildfowl in America, Africa and Europe. Through this I have met the finest bunch of sportsmen one could ever wish to encounter, none of whom I could adequately repay for their kindness and camaraderie over the years.

It is my sincere wish that this book will inspire the young and the young-at-heart to take up the sport of wildfowling and continue its honourable traditions. And for the old hands I hope that *A Pattern of Wings* will recall those days past and those still to come.

CHAPTER I

The Snow Flight

GRAHAM DOWNING

IT SEEMED as though the birds themselves knew that the snow was coming. That evening, as I crouched at flight time in a creek on the salt marsh, the teal had arrived with a special urgency to feed on the little pools of water left by the falling tide. Most of the previous week's ice had gone, and it was only the topmost ridges of the saltings that showed up white under the moonlight – gaunt, skeletal fingers clutching at the inky blackness of the foreshore mud below me as I walked homewards along the sea-wall.

Even as the lights of the village glowed reassuringly ahead a veil was being drawn across the night sky. Thin, high clouds crept out of the west, snuffing the stars one by one, sending a halo round the dimming moon and warning of a change in the weather.

The snow started around midnight. Small, fine flakes at first, falling gently onto the frozen fields and dusting the cottage rooftops. By four in the morning, when I opened the back door and crossed the yard to

4

Teal's kennel, the white powder creaked under my footfalls, and the still, silent air was strangely muffled. Nature held her breath, fearful in the knowledge that this was only just the start of something big, something awesome, a freeze which would turn pond, lake and river to stone, set icebergs afloat on the salt tide and lock land in an iron grip for a month or more.

But it was the sort of weather the wildfowler prays for, and it was with keen anticipation that I loaded the car in readiness for a two-hour drive through a Christmas-card landscape to the fens.

Ours must have been the only car on the road that night, and I made good progress through the sleeping snowbound villages, even though the minor roads were by now becoming treacherous. But at length I reached my destination on the borders of Norfolk and Cambridgeshire and stopped the car under the railway bridge which leads from the rich flat farmland of the fens to the magic world of the washes.

Mounting the bank, I paused for a moment to breathe in the stillness. Black and brooding, the washes spread beneath me, just the distant whistle of a cock wigeon, reaching out of the darkness and the quiet rustle of falling snowflakes scarcely breaking the silence. A raw, rank smell of winter caught my nostrils – an exciting smell, the scent of adventure. I turned to load guns, cartridges and provisions onto my back for the journey across the railway bridge, over the dark waters of the Hundred Foot River and out onto the washes, as Teal leapt around me like a puppy.

The snow was falling more persistently now, but there was not the slightest breath of wind as I trudged for a mile down the frozen bank. It is a long and exhausting walk when one is heavily laden and I was glad to reach the hut. This rugged, weatherbeaten structure, built from driftwood and tarred felt, stands at the head of our marsh as it has done for nearly twenty years, providing a base where the weary fowler can rest and brew coffee or boil a can of soup. I fumbled with the padlock, pulled open the door, then lit a gas lantern before thankfully depositing my gear on the floor of the hut beside me. Looking out across the marsh through the old Land-Rover windscreen which serves as a window, I could see the first fingers of daylight turn the drooping snow clouds from black to grey. It was time to spy out the land.

The best time to shoot the washes is just on the freeze, when the wigeon pile into the last remaining patches of open flooded grazing before moving on to the coast, and it soon became obvious to me that, rather by luck than by good judgement, I had picked more or less perfect conditions. Though most of the marsh was already icebound, a few boggy splashes served by the trickling floodwaters of a running dyke were yet open, and one place, next to a willow clump, was alive with snipe.

My noisy progress, as I crunched through the ice which overlay maybe six inches of water, sent them *scaap-scaap*ing helter-skelter into the gloom, but the few square yards of open marsh which they had vacated seemed an ideal spot in which to lie in ambush, so Teal and I made for the shelter of a nearby frozen willow and built a makeshift hide.

Within minutes the snipe were returning. I was shooting through a gap in the willow branches, picking my snap shots as one would with pigeon on a roost shoot. Before long three snipe were safely in the bag, plus a cock teal, one of a spring of half a dozen that had tried to pitch in almost at my feet before realizing their mistake.

There seemed to be few wigeon on the move. Just the odd pair of birds edged up the washes through the dawn sky as the snow eased temporarily and a pink glow lit up the clouds. One single cock bird, however, swung high over the willows towards me and my shot brought him tumbling to the ground, Teal making her retrieve from the far side of a frozen dyke.

By this time the morning flight was coming to an end, and I made my way back to the hut to brew up a welcome mug of hot soup. Dawn revealed the wintry beauty of the washes, and I stood in the doorway of the hut, scanning the marsh through my binoculars and drinking in the scene.

With their twenty miles of grazing marsh cutting like a narrow finger through the fens, the washes are bounded on each side by great drainage rivers, cut by Dutchmen in bygone days. In the autumn, when the pastures are still green, the place is desolate enough – a stark, uncompromising landscape of three parts sky to one of land, with brimming dykes winking out of an unbroken vista of humpy, tussocky grasses bleached here and there to a thin pale-straw colour.

Then in winter come the floods, spreading far and wide across the flat land, bringing with them tens of thousands of wildfowl which even today can darken the sky. Now the shallow floods had frozen into thin sheets of ice, out of which stood the occasional tussock or bare-branched willow wrapped in a snowy overcoat. Every tint of pink and gold lit up the sky, casting a curious glow which somehow softened the bleakness of the scene, suffusing it with an immense beauty.

From far off came the hoarse coughing of a herd of bullocks on the bank top, and my ear was caught too by the distant but unmistakable whistle of wigeon. On the eastern horizon a fresh bank of cloud threatened more snow before the morning was out.

There is often a second flight about ten o'clock, especially when wind or storm sets the wigeon on edge, and on the far side of the washes I could see a good deal of activity, as small groups of duck rose and settled along the margin of the Delph River, strongly flowing and still free of ice.

As well as my regular game gun, which I had been using all morning, I had brought with me my single 8-bore, a sleek thoroughbred of a gun, with a damascene barrel of chestnut hue and a sweet, smooth action. A wildfowler's dream, it is the sort of weapon that seems to exude romance, adventure and essence of wilderness; simply to use it on the marsh adds spice to a fowling expedition.

The duck traffic which I could see so clearly through the glasses looked promising enough to give the big gun an airing so, with a thermos of hot coffee slipped into my side bag and two pocketfuls of 8-bore shells, I set off under a glowering sky towards the far side of the washes, a freshening breeze now scything into my cheeks. But as Teal and I crunched and slithered our way down towards the Delph I realized that the airborne wigeon which I had spied from the hut were but a fraction of the birds that lay before me. The swollen Delph and the dykes which ran off it were black with wigeon, which, unbelievably, sat tight until, stooping beneath what few scraps of cover there were on the flat, bleak winter washes, I was almost within range.

When the nearest group jumped, about two hundred of them, they hung in the sky, wheeling, turning and sideslipping just beyond my reach, or so they must have thought. But they reckoned without the 8-bore. In an instant the old gun spoke and a cock wigeon was bouncing and sliding on the ice. Working the underlever with smooth efficiency, I got off a second and then a third shot with deadly accuracy before the wigeon realized their mistake.

Quickly Teal gathered the birds and I selected a spot on the snowy river bank where it was possible to find cover amongst a clump of dead nettle stems. Great flat baulks of ice gathered from the margin of the frozen fen were fashioned into a sort of open-topped igloo, a white hide to match the bleak and wintry surroundings of the washes.

Now the snow was upon us once again, this time with a freshening wind behind the pregnant clouds, and visibility closed to about seventy yards. A pulse of excitement coursed through me, the almost electric energy of the hunter who knows that for once, just once, everything is right. Instinctively I felt that in the stinging flakes the birds would be on the move down this, the only open watercourse for a mile, that if I could see a duck it was virtually in range, and that if it was in range then it was dead. For the next hour I enjoyed unforgettable sport.

Within moments the first wigeon came low out of the blizzard. It jinked at the big gun's boom and spun down onto the bank twenty yards distant. Then a pair headed low over me, the cock bird folding to my single shot and skidding a dozen paces across the ice. A mallard and a teal were down next in the river, Teal plunging in with reckless enthusiasm to collect the bobbing birds as they disappeared downstream.

Now the fowl were coming thick and fast out of the blizzard, and the little pile of duck grew beside me. Here a wigeon thumping into the snow of the riverbank, there a pintail crashing on the ice. One bird, a hen teal, went down a strong swimmer and needed a second shot on the water, but Teal worked through the swirling flakes like a black demon and I lost not a single duck.

At about one o'clock the snowstorm ceased and the flight was over. It had finished as quickly as it had started, as if a tap had been turned off or a door closed. I had in any case almost shot out my limited supply of 8-bore cartridges, and it was time to return to the hut. A dozen ducks were removed from my side bag and laid carefully on the small table. Over a welcome ham sandwich and a mug of steaming soup. I inspected each bird, and recalled each shot taken during that magical hour, as sensation slowly returned to frozen feet and numbed fingers.

I had only three more shots that short winter's day. As darkness closed in I took one final walk down to the marsh, this time with the 12-bore. A mallard, quartering across the boundary dyke, I missed clean, but a crossing teal was not so lucky. Failing to connect with the first barrel, I dropped it with the half choke as the little bird stood on its tail and rocketed skywards.

There was a spring in my step that evening as I walked homewards along the bank, for a heavy gamebag is quite a different sort of load from the dead weight of cartridges, of hide, decoys and provisions. A full bag of duck is a burden which any fowler is happy to bear. There was a sparkle too in a labrador's eyes and a contented wag in her tail. Teal had worked all day in bitter snow and ice, plunging in and out of the frozen river with a keenness which had as much of an edge to it as she galloped for that final cock teal as when we had set forth for the morning flight. It takes a special breed, and a special dog, to put up that sort of performance. And she had loved every moment.

The snow continued as I drove home, and over the next couple of days arctic winds gripped the coast in an iron frost. Within a week a wildfowling ban was declared and I had virtually no more shooting that season. Not that I minded overmuch, for the birds needed a respite during those Siberian conditions, and in any case I had been lucky enough to have picked the flight of the season.

CHAPTER II

Moon Flight

MICHAEL SHEPHARD

T HERE WAS a time when I was deeply in love with darkness and the growing dusk was like a door opening on another world. As a child I had never feared the dark and as I grew I embraced the night like a friend and an ally in many of my adventures with rod, gun, nets and wires. Then when the world erupted I found no little exhilaration in night patrols and, whilst only a fool or zombie would deny being afraid at times or glorify war at others, I know that many will know what I mean. If nothing more, I learned to use darkness as a cloak and continued to do so long after hostilities had ceased.

I must admit that I have always preferred to share my sport with others; but, whether fishing a fly for sea-trout after dark or lying in wait for wigeon or the grey geese during various phases of moonlight, the night is another door which closes behind you, shutting out the prosaic world of normality and even the best of friends, who are otherwise with you somewhere on marsh or mud or beside another

10

pool farther along the river. And if you are to use the gifts of darkness to the full you must learn to improve and develop your own powers of hearing and sight and to move with as much confidence and silence as the terrain allows.

One night I set out across the Halvergate Marshes towards a point halfway between the sea wall of Breydon Water and the long, straight road from Great Yarmouth to Acle, and I was on my own – something I was later to regret after enjoying a flight which I can never forget and, at the same time, can never share with anyone.

It was full dark as I left the car and an hour yet before the eastern horizon began to herald the rising moon. To all intents the marshes were empty and I walked across the familiar wilderness of winter grass quite quickly, with eyes acclimatizing to new conditions and ears attuning themselves to the noises of the night. My passage was sufficiently unannounced to extract a harsh *craank* from a heron waiting beside the rhine and I was just able to see it embodied against the sky as it flapped slowly away.

At the bottom of the first marsh I turned along the rhine to find a ligger – one of those narrow planks which provide easy passage from one grazing to another in summer and become a hazard to be negotiated with great care in winter. The one I found was dry and unfrosted and, with the brief aid of a pencil torch, I crossed it with no great difficulty. An equally easy crossing of a second drain brought me to one of the areas of grass which Robin Harrison had earlier told me the geese were using.

In those days I worked for the British Field Sports Society in Victoria Street and, with one of the anti Bills coming up in the Commons, the past weeks had been hectic. This was a very welcome break and the only pity was that I had driven straight up from London with no time to pick up the dog, while my old friend the Breydon watcher was unable to join me on this adventure.

I walked about the marsh and soon found evidence of recent use by geese as I sensed a subtle lightening of the horizon beyond the warm glow above the town. Robin had warned me that the tide would not encourage the geese to leave the Scrobie Sands until after dawn, but a waning moon was due to make an appearance for several hours before daylight.

It was then that I came across something which forced my plan to change: a solid lump loomed up in the faint light – a mass which looked much like the great outcrops of granite that lie across the face of West

11

Country moors. This mass, however, was steaming and I realized that not all the store cattle had been removed from the marsh. Anyway, even if the whitefronts were happy to share the grass with the steers, I could not risk shooting anywhere near Mr Myra Sutton's cattle (or maybe they were Denny Wright's) and another spot had to be found without delay.

Fortunately the cloud mass was denser than expected and the moon's influence on the scene delayed long enough for me to negotiate two more narrow planks to reach another grazing area favoured by both the geese and our guns in previous winters. There I found my old 'hide' – a five-barred gate hanging crazily from one stout post and partly secured to another by binder twine. Why is it that on those Norfolk marshes heavy gates which securely pen thousands of grazing beasts through the summer always seem to hang their heads in shame, neglected and in need of therapy, during the winter months?

As I placed the heavy gamebag beside the post I realized that I had overdressed; the cold was less than I had expected. But it would be foolish now to dispense with any layer of clothing as my body cooled off after the last hurried trek across the fields. As it happened there was no noticeable cooling period: as I reached deep into the pocket of my camouflaged smock, toying with the idea of lighting up my pipe, a large shape appeared on softly silent wings above my head and my friend the heron settled gently on the grass a few yards on the other side of the gate.

I fully expected the bird to walk across to the rhine, but it remained still and I could only guess that it had chosen a point where rats or water voles crossed the marsh from my ditch to another which ran at right angles from it. Through the bars of the gate the heron was visible to me – its head and neck and upper body clearly so against the skyline, the rest only a vague blur melding with the marsh grasses.

From the fishing harbour came the sound of a ship's horn as a herring drifter came back to port. From the road the sound of a car, its lights cutting a shaft through the darkness behind me – a doctor called urgently to some crisis, a midwife brought suddenly from her bed to a premature delivery, or a guest driving homewards after late-night revelry. Such idle conjecture ended abruptly as the sound I had been hoping to hear came clear and absolutely unmistakable across the soft air – at first distantly as the leading skeins of geese drove across the night, then silence for a while, then a sudden clamour much closer than expected, and high.

They were surprisingly high considering the relatively short distance the birds had flown from the sand-bar and the first large group passed directly over me unseen, heading up marsh towards Reedham. The second skein, however, were lower along the same path and I glimpsed them, but too briefly for a shot. But I had moved in anticipation and, with another eldritch shriek, my feathered fisherman flew off. I am sure the heron first gave rise to talk of witches and broomsticks.

There was a gap after the first two flights of geese, but it did not seem so as the rising clamour of more skeins came across the marsh while the voices of the first faded, and suddenly I heard the whisper of pinions as several small parties dropped low above the sleeping cattle and began to whiffle around that grazing ground. Then there was a silence beneath the continuing chorus from the upper air, followed by a contented soft muttering, and I knew that some whitefronts, at least, were down on the marsh I had originally chosen. This was not unduly worrying for anyone knowing the ways of the geese which feed across such wide expanses of marsh. Under the moon the birds often grow restless and begin 'rhine-hopping' and small groups can present themselves to the gunner at any time while there are geese on the marsh.

I was pondering this as a bunch of seven did just that – looming silently out of the gloom towards the road swinging into silhouette against the moon-illumined screen of cloud. They were close enough for my Grant and its 2 ½-inch cartridges of No. 5 shot. I straightened my crouched, cramped body above the gate and took two cool and calculated shots and was rewarded by my first two geese of a new season. The birds fell no more than thirty yards from the gateway and I ran across to recover them, then back to the gate as wings filled the night with their sound and patterned the sky about me.

A single bird passed within feet of me, too close for a shot, but a jumbled mass of some twenty geese gave another fine chance as they climbed and crossed my line of vision. Again two hit the grass and I let them lie where they fell as the engagement hotted up and fresh skeins came in after the others departed. In fact, not a lot of opportunity presented itself, but geese were milling about the marshes all the time and it seemed that the whole of Robin's estimated 800 whitefronts had come in from the sands.

Above the babble of voices I knew so well and during the silences which fell on the marsh from time to time I had listened for a different tongue – the unmistakable call of the pink-footed geese, of which Robin had told me some 300 were sharing the roost and the grazing with their cousins from Novaya Zemlya. But the pinks always chose another marsh and showed great preference for the Bure marshes on the other side of the Acle road, often flying the line of the river as far as the Stracey Arms before turning back across the fields and dykes. As I say, I had been listening with one ear for the wild cacophony of the pinks, but it had not come and I guessed that they had given up the moonlight lark and would arrive with the dawn or a little later when the tide drove them off the roost.

The excitement (and there is as much of that in listening to the geese as they explore the marsh and listening for them when all is silence as there is at that moment when they are coming to you, when the skein is upon you or skipping across a rhine way out to the flank) continued for some time and, as the part-moon rode high and the cloud cover thinned, showing up many geese which had hitherto been disembodied noises in the night.

In the course of those two hours I picked a high-flying singleton and managed my third right-and-left, while a huge company of wigeon swept across the bright cloud screen and left three duck and a drake behind. But I was subsequently humbled by clear misses at a couple of mallard, a single goose and a family party of eight whitefronts, from which one tumbled to the ground after flying on some way. By the time I had managed to find and dispatch the wounded bird the sun was rising as the moon dropped below the land. There was, indeed, no real dawn.

No pink-footed geese, either! When I reached the car with my load, having dropped the lot in a ditch to take a golden plover on the way, I was tempted to cross the river marsh and await the tide; but I was whacked and just sat in the car and watched the other geese come in before I headed up the long straight towards the Stracey Arms, a steaming bath and the exhausted fowler's reward, a hearty breakfast.

14

CHAPTER III

Goose Music

BB

I WAS with my old fowling companion Major Charles Oakey, MC. He used a 16-bore on both game and geese and was a good wildfowler, knowing how to take cover. This ability had once saved his life, when, during one of the bloodiest battles of the First World War, with a machine-gun picking off his men all round him, he crawled up behind the only cover he could see, a bunch of dead thistles.

With us was Bob Kennedy, the Tay wildfowler. His friend 'over the hill', as he put it, had the pinks eating in his barley field and Kennedy assured us that we should get some sport when the moon rose.

It was a bitter January night with snow lying. On preliminary daylight recces we had found the snow strewn with the little rolled green droppings of the geese and feathers on dark melted patches where they had sat down after feeding.

We reached the ground about 7 p.m. The moon was well up in a clear starlit sky – the very worst sky for night shooting. I settled down on a bare patch where the wind had blown the snow away. Here I would be less visible, though wild geese – sharp-eyed as they are – cannot see all that well in the dark. Charles and Kennedy placed themselves away to my right at the far end of the field and we settled down to wait.

That silent moonlit landscape, the starlit sky, a light in a distant farmhouse over the burn, the thin wailing of a green plover, all were noted, all etched in memory.

A hare came loppiting, ears in a V, caught our wind, and was away like a startled stag. Something brushed my cheek, ever so gently. It was a snowflake. Looking north, I saw a bank of cloud advancing. Just what we wanted! Soon the sky above was a pearly marbled veil through which the full moon shone like a pale disc. It was snowing quite hard but I could not see the flakes, only felt them on my face and saw my shoulders turning white.

Then came on the ear that distant magic music, the sound of the hounds of Herne the Hunter, as the old shepherds used to say as they minded their hill sheep at lambing time. The music came and went like bells upon the wind as the skeins turned and weaved over the strath. They had had a long and wearisome climb over the mountains and now they were free-wheeling onto their feeding ground.

Louder the music! The safety catch slips forward and there above come the gliding black shapes, wings all set, not one wagging, all gliding and wheeling. At my shot the dark silhouette I fired at seemed to swell like a balloon. There was a resounding thump on the snow. At the same instant other shots rang out from Charles and Bob and distinct snow bumps announced that everyone had had success.

That night the skeins kept coming in, not in one great mass but in little parties. It would be tiresome to describe each shot, each miss. When we had seven down we called it a night and gathered up the slain.

Then we retired to the local inn. It was closed but Bob was a friend of the landlord and we were soon ushered into a warm bar, a roaring fire and some glasses of the hard stuff. It was right to celebrate for it had been my first experience of shooting under the moon and we had been extraordinarily lucky with the weather. The snowstorm had saved the night. It was still snowing when we left the inn, at heaven knows what late hour, and went back to HQ very happy men.

There have been other moon flights, not so successful in numbers of birds shot. There have been wonderful flights at dawn in northerly gales and snow. There have been nights when I have crawled among the reeds and had feeding geese all within reach, all guzzling away and buzzing like bees.

I cannot believe that the daytime pheasant or partridge shooter has so many vivid memories. They are surely the prerogative of the shore gunner, or perhaps the stalker on the hill.

CHAPTER IV

Winter Whitefront

ALAN JARRETT

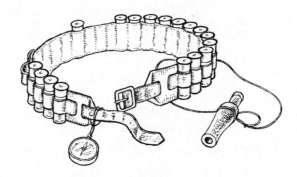

I T WAS with a feeling of intense relief that I finally stepped out onto the snow-encrusted roadway after over an hour of tortuously slow progress. Horror then on reaching my destination to find that there was nowhere to park, for the snow was piled high all about, and it took some frantic work with the shovel before the situation was saved and I was off the road.

What a relief! Also a fine tribute to the amazingly tenacious little green minivan that I had reached that destination at all. How I would extricate the van from the tiny niche I had carved for it on my return from the flight did of course cross my mind – but the flight was of paramount importance and later would be plenty soon enough to worry about getting home.

It is now possible to look back on such times with fond affection, for only a constant shortage of cash necessitated the ownership of such a tatty vehicle anyway. Now today's high-performance hatchback would probably fail to get through at all in the face of such adversity. But in those days I had shot comparatively few duck and like most of my kind was endlessly in search of that one red-letter day. I had to get through.

This day the conditions were absolutely perfect – all the textbooks said so – and I was alone with the whole wide vista of the salt marsh before me, with a draining tide leaving behind a freshly thawed banquet for the duck to flock upon. So it was with great enthusiasm that I set off along the open sea-wall where the snow lay deep and the wind blew bitterly. The dog snorted playfully amid the whiteness, and this time I felt sure that I could not fail.

The waders were coming through in great clouds to twist and wheel with apparent joy at spying the emerging muds which were their lifeblood; the shore was vibrantly alive and full of birds, and it was a pleasure to be out despite the cold. The higher and middle reaches of the salt marsh were deep in snow, with vast flat sheets and craggy blocks of ice littered all about where a succession of tides had done half a job of thawing, only for the next frost to freeze everything solid again. On the outer edge the salting gave no hint of the severity of the conditions, but lay cloistered in a miracle world of its own.

Only after tucking myself into a convenient creek bottom, so as to remain hidden for the most part from the sharp-eyed duck, did I begin to appreciate fully just how cold it really was; the wind whipped down out of the north with a wicked venom and slashed at any exposed flesh with an icy knife. The creek did shelter me from the worst of the blast, but it was still awfully cold and grew colder still as I cooled down after the exertions of digging and walking. To the west the sky was fairly bright, with even a trace of blue here and there, but off to the north and east there was a brooding darkening which could only herald more snow.

But where were the duck which I had expected to pile in as though there were no tomorrow? A few small packs of wigeon were working the receding tideline, while the occasional high-flying mallard or low-dashing teal put in an appearance, but there was little coming to the salting while the light remained good. Either the duck were not as hungry as they might have been or else they were all off feeding in other parts. I suspected the latter, and the dearth of birds caused the cold to bite deeper still.

Blast! Three teal overhead and gone before I could react. More teal, then a few wigeon, swinging into the lush greenery farther along the shore, and with wigeon now moving purposefully it was obvious that the flight had started earlier than I had dared hope. Four wigeon were hopelessly missed as they came across the wind, for I had stiffened up and found it difficult to move freely. A rigorous bout of arm-waving thereafter helped to get the circulation going again and to take a few of the creases out of my coat at the same time.

Two duck came slowly right to me from the east at almost zero feet, and it transpired that they were shoveler as they began to climb and turn away in alarm. Having yet to shoot a shoveler at that time I immediately fluffed the shot as they began to rear up on the wind, but connected with the duck on the second attempt, sending her spinning down. A joyful time this, studying the strange corpse and delighting in what now seems a small enough victory. In common with most wildfowlers I still have not shot more than a couple of dozen shoveler, and these turned up mostly on the brackish marshes close to the shore. They are an interesting variation to the bag on the odd occasion when they appear – but never a species which can be counted on.

A handsome mallard drake came in off the sea to pass me high and wide – the sort of half chance which is all too easy to miss. But his head went back and he fell in a great arc to land way back in the salting beyond the snowline. Here at the best of times lay a dog-defying tangle of broken-stemmed sea aster and spartina, but now a foot of snow lay on top and it was a nightmare for the dog. Obviously the drake had plummeted through the snow into the salting below and would be almost impossible to find. The dog hunted gamely enough, but not surprisingly could make nothing of it. In my turn I stomped tetchily about, frustrated that I seemed about to lose my reward for so fine a shot; yet by a stroke of good fortune I spotted a hole in the packed snow and reached in to find the mallard stone dead beneath.

By now the light was fading and the first flutters of snow were falling onto the shore. Many packs of duck were now on the move and I shot a cock teal, which again fell back in the snow, although this time without penetrating the white layer, providing an easy retrieve for the dog. Another teal, this time a hen, fell onto the thawed area and this too was swiftly brought to hand. Then there were a few shots at surprisingly wary wigeon, none of which connected, and as the snow fell heavier still it was obvious that the flight could not last much longer in the rapidly fading light.

It had been a strange flight in many ways, with birds coming in sporadic fashion and not as hungrily as I might have wished for. Yet four duck, including that first shoveler, were not to be sneezed at and I would certainly have settled for that score before setting out.

Another teal flared into the wind at my first shot, then set its wings into a glide at the second to disappear into the gloom. Blast! Peering into the wind, I had to try to judge where the bird might have fallen – if indeed it had come down at all – which was a fairly hopeless task but had to be attempted. It turned out to be a very happy decision.

Once out of the creek I was in a different world of tugging wind and whirling snow, while the blackness closed in all around. The salting was a wet and stodgy mess of snow and mud, creeks still gurgling at the ebb, with the ghostly plaints of grey plover and curlew somewhere out near the tideline – a mirage from some dreamy wildfowling legend.

Trudging onto the estimated line of the teal, I set the dog to work. She plunged and spluttered through the gloom while I kept a sharp eye open just in case. The occasional burst of wild whistling presaged the vague silhouette of some racing wigeon pack or the faint stuttering of some roaming mallard as they swung round prior to a greedy bout of guzzling amid the slushy margins before the frost came to deny them.

The dog came to me for guidance, and we made off for a further fifty yards or so to the east before resuming the search. Here the salting was broken by larger creeks cutting out to sea, with spartina beds as smaller isolated islands. I squatted on one of these, huddled against the snow, while listening to her fitful dashing search.

Soon from the north-west came a flicker of lighter music on the wind, at first half-heard, half-imagined; then no mistaking the sound of geese, so that the stomach fluttered and trembling hands sought heavy loads for the magnum. Now they were closer, the high-pitched chime of the whitefronts pressing down on me from above in a crescendo of sound before the wind swept them past unseen in the night. Their voices were soon drowned by the storm, so that nothing was left save the fall of the snow and the sporadic pitter-patter of the teal hunter.

To be a wildfowler who has yet to kill a grey goose leaves a void which may threaten to engulf you, as it did me now that the ultimate quarry had been and gone. I brushed the snow from the magnum and then realized that it was over. The geese had gone, and the teal was obviously not to be found.

Geese again. I gave a snort, for I did not believe that these would be any more visible than the squadron which had gone before. Nonetheless, the optimistic wildfowler will bid the dog be still, grip the gun ever tighter and peer into the black above as if to will the quarry to appear.

21

The magic of the shot then – the snow which flays the upturned cheeks; the sighting, be it ever so brief, of part of a larger company; the quick swing; the shot, and the hard punch of the heavy load; the yelling cries of alarm as the skein scrambles for height, geese racing on with the wind in their rumps. A pause then – for an age, it seems – before the unseen bird thwacks the mud and the heart leaps with unbridled joy.

Then we were off, man and dog alone in the night to find the goose huddled as if against the cold. But there was no feeling in that lifeless form; it could not feel the wind or the cold, or my excitedly trembling hands. At last!

The walk back was akin to an ecstatic floating dream. I barely sensed the wind or snow but was well aware of the bundle of duck and the goose, which even combined seemed to weigh but little. Soon the van beckoned in the eerie, snowy night, with the snow deeper than ever. But the engine started first time, and the shovel was still in working order, so I knew that I would get home somehow. With a smile I laid the goose on the van floor, ruffled the dog's neck affectionately, and started to dig.

The edge of the loch Geoffrey Campbell-Black

Wigeon return with the sunrise *Julian Novorol*

First arrivals at evening flight *Jonathan Yule*

Pintail under the moon *John Paley*

Teal following the creek, Hamford Water, Essex *Julian Novorol*

Floodwater, The Avon, Hampshire *Geoffrey Campbell-Black*

Dawn arrivals, wigeon with the tide at low ebb *Julian Novorol*

Mallard over Stoke Marsh on the Medway *Ian Phipps*

CHAPTER V

White-Out

NEOFLAK

THE WINTER of 1981 suddenly turned nasty around 10 December. Iron-hard frosts and moaning nor'easterlies, which solidified soil and water and cut through clothing like a chain-saw, showed that the ice-spirit had clamped firm hold and claimed his season with a vengeance.

The advent of this mini ice age made me feel very pleased as I went about my daily work. A few days and nights of this would concentrate the minds of wildfowl wonderfully, especially duck, and help to civilize them somewhat. The trouble was that it went on too long. By the time I was able to get two days off, the freeze had lasted ten days and there was no sign of a let-up. A fowling halt would surely be called shortly. There was no time to lose.

As I parked the car near the sea-wall at dawn on the first of my two planned expeditions, I noticed that the wind had changed overnight and was blowing from the south. I therefore revised the planned siting of my hide as, together with Storm, I began the long, winding walk to the distant island out in the estuary. This island, out in the Medway, can no longer be shot, so I'm glad that I took every opportunity to do so when I could. Such is progress! It was, and I am sure still is, an excellent duck marsh on its day, as there is food in abundance for dabblers and divers alike at most stages of the tide.

It was still very cold walking along the washed-out, tide-wracked causeway which joined the mainland with my destination, but the wind was no longer dry and keen; rather it now had a grey, damp clamminess to it. Often I had to flounder through knee-deep mud as our journey progressed, for large sections of the rough brick and flintstone base had been eroded and carried away by the tide in its ceaseless battle to level everything in its path. As we drew nearer the ancient sea-wall which girdled the island, I could see a grey-white mantle of frost and newly fallen snow covering the top of the sea rampart, above the high-water mark. A little more snow had fallen here overnight than at home. Around the tops of the small islets of spartina grass, which the causeway snaked around, the retreating tide had deposited small, thin sheets of cat ice, which tilted at crazy angles as the water had left them. Small, ragged groups of knot, dunlin and redshank fed voraciously on the exposed mud before this intertidal lifeline froze again.

Parties of duck, mostly teal, rose frequently from dry creek beds and odd pools left by the tide. They were freshly arrived from the European seaboard, pushed across the North Sea by the freezing weather in their quest for food.

With hide poles in hand, I climbed over the island sea-wall after half an hour's steady plod. I surveyed the scene. The wall, which once totally enclosed the marsh, had been broken and breached in several places by the great storm and exceptional spring tide of 1953, notably in its south-western corner. The area of salting and bisecting gutters runs to roughly 800 acres, dominated by twin mounds looking like grey, greenish loaves, which rise out of the surrounding flatness, perhaps 600 yards apart. These two 'fortresses' are excellent flighting positions, but a gamble played maybe for the highest stake if occupied during an oncoming freak spring tide.

I moved down the eastern side of the marsh, towards its southern boundary. The midday tide I knew would be a high one and with the stiff wind now blowing this might be the only sheltered spot the duck could find as the water rose. Around the marsh's perimeter, little dark shapes busied themselves making hides – other fowlers like myself making the most of the rare combination of tide and weather. The odd flat-sounding shot thudded across the flat pan of salting from the opposite wall as teal in ones and twos began zipping through the great gap in the sea defences low over the making water, the turning tide inducing this undulating, twisting, spontaneous aerial helter-skelter.

I chose a spot near the south-eastern corner of the banking, where the side of the wall is shadowy and undercut by the tide. Within ten minutes the hide building was complete, plastic scrim hung and the finishing touches made with the aid of seaweed and a couple of wooden crates which were lying where they had been left by a previous high water. My eight decoys were deployed in two small groups in front of my ambush, about fifteen yards apart, one in a deepish creek, to take advantage of the early flood, the other anchored a little to the left on a piece of higher mud where they would float when the sea aster roots were awash. As I heeled the last of the decoy pegs into the ooze, I looked back at the hide. For once it appeared perfect, low and hidden in shadow. In fact, I had to study the wall's dark contour carefully from twenty-five yards out to notice it at all.

We settled into it and I made Storm as comfortable as was possible, given the conditions, which was not very comfortable at all, as he sat on my empty decoy sack, which covered a pile of dead sea lavender and other assorted plant wrack brought in by the tide, whilst I perched on an old plastic barrel and made quick adjustments to the rim of our ambush.

At various other points around the rim of the wall other die-hards were doing the same when, as if by a given signal, by common consent, all the human forms which up till then had been busy scurrying about hide-making disappeared. No one this day had long to wait. Icy tendrils of water stirred the keels of my decoys and, as if at this sign, wigeon curled across the marsh, now rising and turning, now banking into the raw wind and planing low over innumerable filling creeks. The skirl of the ducks and the banshee whistling of the drakes was clearly heard in the chill, grey air and I took one out of the first wedge, which came straight into the decoys with no preliminary circling. Storm rushed out and plucked him where he had fallen, white breast up on the swelling tide. Before he returned with his prize, my fourth shot punched two out of the next pack, so intent were they in finding shelter and feeding away from the open water. One bird, a drake, fell dead, whilst the other, a duck, paddled away parallel to the wall and crept into a clump of spiky reeds, while I watched, waiting and unseen.

Storm and I hurried around the perimeter of the little bay formed by the angle of the wall, stopping to collect the saffron-headed drake bobbing at the tide's edge on the way. The young eager brown muzzle reappeared from the middle of the ice-encrusted spikes with the duck squarely held in his jaws. A satisfying end to a lucky shot. My esteem for both him and my new magnum grew as we quickly disappeared again into our ambush.

The wind strengthened, slush ice lipped the fringes of the incoming tide. It was bitterly cold now. Duck, waders and brent geese made continuous weaving patterns as they skimmed the steel-grey waves, their formations undulating in the raw wind, their masses now darkening, now turning to light grey as they milled and turned endlessly – the exact picture depicted in treasured engravings of long ago. Shooting was now continuous around the rim of the island. In small parties and large flocks, duck were flying and pitching in their hundreds everywhere on the heaving tide. I shot and shot. My kills-to-cartridges ratio was blown to hell and still they came. Ice formed on Storm's chest as he plunged into that arctic sea again and again, each time upon his return shaking himself free of the congealing wetness with a sound like thin chandeliers being rattled together as the ice formed on his long coat.

Despite the breathless action and excitement, the terrible wind had frozen me to the marrow and Storm's teeth chattered incessantly as he quivered to gain body heat. Duck or no duck, we both badly needed a warm-up, so, leaving the hide, I quickly rolled over the top of the wall and together we jogged along the tide's edge on the outside of the marsh so as not to disturb others shooting until some semblance of circulation returned to my numbed limbs.

I had barely turned round after rubbing the dog down with handfuls of dry, bleached grass when a movement over the top of the embankment caught my eye and had my gun frantically seeking a mark among six wind-tossed pintail over my head. I managed to fire once and an exquisite, streamlined drake folded up, whilst the rest banked and sped away in neck-stretching headlong flight. The tide had now turned, the erstwhile eager waters receding fast. Still it seemed that every fowl in creation was on the wing. The pile of slain stashed in my hide grew. I no longer fired at teal; they were too commonplace and my supply of cartridges was nearing exhaustion. I concentrated on wigeon, pintail and the occasional mallard, trying to pick my birds.

As the short day neared its end and the light began to fade, we left the sea-bank and walked out some little way into the low interior of the marsh across the drying salting and hid in a deep creek, its hard, red clay bottom giving firm footing. My last four cartridges netted two final wigeon. With these in hand, I climbed over the lip of the gutter to begin bagging up. It had grown dark quite suddenly. Great billowing clouds cut out the twilight and I fancied the wind had veered a trifle to the west and was strengthening rapidly.

With the aid of my pocket torch I tied the duck in bunches, stuffed them into the bag overflowing after winding in my decoys, filled the side pockets of my coat and finally hung them in bundles festooned around my neck. All twenty-six of them. I felt I could hardly walk! Looking at my watch, I noticed that it had taken me an hour to pack up. The other fowlers seemed to have gone. Last again! It was then, as we walked slowly around the wall towards the start of the seaward end of the causeway, that something wet and freezing touched my cheek.

Snow! I flicked on my torch, turning slowly to face the buffeting wind, bent over with the weight of my load. The air was a solid, falling, white mass. I began the causeway walk. Looking back again after crossing the main creek bed under the sea-wall, I was alarmed to find that the tall, triangular navigation symbol had disappeared. This was always visible close up even on the darkest night, a sure bearing and aid to direction. After another five-minute plod, the blizzard really started. I stopped, totally lost, enveloped in this white cocoon. The causeway and surrounding marsh were gone, hidden under this sudden, driven mantle. The way twisted and turned upon itself and the mud to either side was evil and unwalkable. There was also the question of the returning tide.

Alone in this howling maelstrom, terrified now to the core of my being, I began to panic. Then Storm nudged against my waders, 'Come on boy, show me the way, or we've had it,' I shouted to him above the moaning wind. In a moment of inspired desperation, I tied a length of plastic string around his wet neck and wound the other end around my wrist. My faithful friend, head down, plodded forwards. Never for a yard did he wander from the invisible track. With the death-trap mud to either side and the flooding tide behind, he steadily led me through the impenetrable curtain of snow.

At long last I felt the way begin to slope upwards, we were off. I fell to my knees and, putting my arms around him, thanked him for my deliverance. There before us lay the car, half buried beneath a four-foot drift. No matter, home at last and blessed safety. Was there ever such a duck flight? Was there ever such a wonderful dog?

CHAPTER VI

Wigeon Under the Moon

DAVID ASHENDEN

A S SOON as the war was over and I had returned to normal life from the army, I arranged a visit to Holy Island. At that time superb wildfowling was free for all on the vast mudflats between the island and the mainland. The area was particularly noted for its punt gunning and wigeon flighting.

I travelled north on the night sleeper from King's Cross as petrol rationing was still on. I was very nearly thrown off the train at dawn when the sleeping car attendant discovered that I was sharing my bunk with my brown Sussex spaniel. Apparently I had broken every by-law governing the carriage of livestock by rail. She should have been consigned to the guard's van, tied to a dog rail among the luggage. However, as I was shortly due to change trains at Newcastle matters were allowed to rest as the bitch was virtually invisible among the blankets.

The trip from the little station at Beal across the bay to Holy Island was an adventure in itself. The pre-war Austin 20 chugged through water up to its running boards, the driver navigating by the line of poles marking the only safe course. There was no permanent causeway in those days and he had to be careful not to stray into the numerous patches of soft mud.

After settling in at the pub which was to be my headquarters for the next four days, I wandered down to the little quay on the edge of the mudflats. Brent geese were floating seawards on the falling tide and bunches of wigeon sat riding the gentle swell farther out. The quay was deserted except for a man sitting with his legs dangling over the edge. After passing the time of day he informed me that he and his mate were going after the black geese (as he called them) with the big gun. Presently, he let himself down on the mud and walked to a small shed, where his mate was mounting the stanchion gun on a double punt.

I met Bob, my guide, about half past three on that December afternoon by the little straw stack behind the quay, provided for the use of wildfowlers by an understanding farmer. Anyone was welcome to draw a bundle before setting out for use in his hide. 'Hide' is not quite the word, as I was to learn, because one had to settle for the bottom of a gutter or, at best, one of the boxes shaped like coffins sunk permanently in the mud by the locals. I was to be accommodated in an absentee fowler's 'coffin'. First it had to be emptied of water. I fished about in the cold water for the old handbowl used as a bailer. When most of the water had gone the straw was laid in the bottom, and one kept surprisingly dry lying prone there.

On the way out I had noticed several fowlers going their separate ways, each submerged under his bundle. I seemed to be the only one accompanied by a dog. Few wildfowlers in those days thought it necessary to keep a dog to retrieve the slain.

After I had taken my instructions Bob disappeared into a gutter about 500 yards away. All the others had vanished too. It was a strange feeling lying there below the level of the mudflats. I felt suddenly very much alone – and somewhat apprehensive. Was it certain that Bob would be able to find me in the dark when it was time to go? If he could find me, had he calculated the tide correctly and was he competent to guide me back to civilization through the maze of runnels and gutters separating us from the shoreline? Such stupid thoughts ran through my mind as I lay there, my only companion the wet dog between my knees.

The moon lifted above the horizon and pointed a silver finger of light across the sea towards us. The mudflats glistened in the moonlight.

Apprehension turned to pleasurable anticipation. My thoughts were interrupted by a faint whistle. Wigeon over the sea! The evocative *whee-oo* of one cock is enough to set the adrenalin going and I lost all thoughts of being drowned at sea. There were wigeon under the moon flying all about me but none was visible in the bright unshaded light. Cloud cover was lacking except for a small white patch in front. Six shapes were silhouetted as they flashed across and were gone before I could sit up, let alone raise my gun. The bitch quivered and sank back into the straw.

After that first burst of activity the only sound one could hear was the gently soughing of the sea pushing forwards on the turn of the tide. Half an hour had gone by when I realized that the moon's silver finger was no longer visible on the water. The strengthening breeze was bringing more cloud, and with luck there would be sufficient backcloth to silhouette any duck that might come my way.

The silence was broken by more wigeon calling as they flew in from the sea. The swish of their wings was audible as they passed as yet unseen. The sounds were utterly confusing; birds seemed everywhere. I lost all sense of direction trying to locate their approach; sometimes they came from behind, sometimes across my front, sometimes head-on. I did see one bunch momentarily, but they vanished before I could raise my gun.

As more clouds covered the sky I was able to see approaching birds earlier and in time to fire. After several abortive shots I decided that it was only practical to take on birds passing over my left shoulder, as it were. The right-handed Shot can swing the gun more easily from right to left when sitting down and is less likely to stop the swing at the moment of firing.

My first success came with a single wigeon approaching at just the right angle and a clean kill restored a little of my lost confidence. The duck crashed down behind me with a mighty splash in the soft mud. The bitch could only mark by the sound but she was away in the right direction. She returned with the rather muddy bird, covering me with mud as she shook herself before she climbed aboard. In the short time that flight lasted I almost emptied my cartridge belt. Altogether I gathered five wigeon, an average of about one in five.

I was relieved to hear Bob splashing towards me as the sea seemed to be getting uncomfortably close. The gathering mist concerned Bob more than the encroaching sea. There was no smudge of shoreline to be seen. However, we weaved our way through the intricacies of runnels and gutters and arrived safely at the quay, where a few fellow fowlers were waiting.

There was concern about a young lad who was still out in what was now a foggy night. A couple of shots were fired and there was relief when an answering shout was heard. The boy said he was on the wrong side of the long gutter and could not find the safe crossing. It was rapidly filling so Bob walked out into the fog to guide him over. All was well in the end except for one very wet lad who had misjudged the tide while searching for a lost duck.

After supper that night the talk in the bar-parlour was of fowling in 'the old days', of the time when the great amateurs, like Abel Chapman and his puntsman, Selby Allison, stalked the black geese and the wigeon with the big gun. They described some of the exploits of the bird collectors who, in their day, were also great exponents of coastal shooting.

I was told too of a night around the turn of the century when a wife of one of the professional wildfowlers burst into this little bar-parlour with the dramatic words: 'My man's not come – he's still out.' The company knew what that meant, for the tide was half full and the mist was on the mudflats.

Without a word the men went out. When they came to the raised part of the mudflats known as the mussel scaup they heard a faint shout. There was a sort of depression all round it and the water was waist-deep and spilling over the mud behind them. One of the party was pretty sure where the man was; the mussel scaup was a favourite place for flighting in those days. He plunged through the water and with tremendous good fortune found the stranded man, who had slipped and broken his ankle as he came away from this highly dangerous place. The rescuer picked up the injured man with a fireman's lift and carried him to where the party had gathered. Willing hands helped both men through the deep water and between them they carried the injured one back to the shore in thick fog.

CHAPTER VII

Ice Morning

JOHN HUMPHREYS

T HE FROST did more than hold; it gripped with the icy fist of chain-mail. It took a hefty clout to break the ice in the bullocks' water trough, and the tumbled clods on the ten-acre ploughing – such heavy going in milder times – now had the hardness and unpredictability of crazy paving after an earthquake.

A teenager with his first magnum, his first dog and his first full season of unaccompanied shooting is not the best judge of what does or does not constitute a promising wildfowling morning. He cares not for the omens; his alarm clock is redundant, for long before its shrill command he is wide awake, lest the sunrise catch him napping. He is non-selective, setting forth whatever the weather, in spite of the headshakings and admonitions of old hands who aver that 'It's far too calm this morning. Not worth bothering. Think I'll have a lie-in.' Such a collect is heresy: the man on the marsh is more likely to get a shot than the man snuggled down in his eiderdown and snoring fit to wake the dead.

I was that lad who, long before dawn, wheeled out his father's old college Hercules, and hung his BSA three-inch in the Fenman's patent bike gun carriage. This device allowed the barrels to hang in a metal hook fixed to the handlebars and the wrist of the weapon to swing in a leather strap fixed under the saddle post. I could and did ride many a mile hardly aware that I was carrying such an awkward burden.

The stars were diamond chips on a jeweller's velvet tray; the tyres scrunched through frozen puddles, and once I skidded perilously at the head of the lane where the road right-angled down to the marsh. My breath puffed out white and smoky as from a cigar; lungs and nose burned with the cold, cheeks glowed, toes and fingertips already were numb, despite all that good oiled wool and Dunlop could do to protect them.

Then I was there, pulling into the rough grass where the old stack stood, leaning my machine against its hairy flank, standing a moment to absorb the new silence created by my sudden cessation of motion. At my side, listening just as intently, stood a pale yellow labrador named Ajax, after the Greek warrior and not, may I point out in defence of his memory, a certain proprietary brand of foaming sink-cleaner. From puppyhood he had been trained to lope along, his nose level with the sturdy back wheel of the Hercules, his ground-eating stride clocking up many hundreds of miles in his ten years of shooting with me.

Small sounds now became clear, were recognized and dismissed. An owl hooted tremulously from the oaks in the meadow, a farm dog barked, a cockerel crowed to the dawn he sensed was imminent. Then, far away, a cock wigeon whistled; as if in answer a mallard quacked stridently – *kaar kaar kaar kaar* – both sounds more than encouragement to break my reverie and have me unsleeving the gun, shaking out the strap of my canvas bag and tramping off along the familiar track.

Ice fringed the stems of the tall grasses and water docks where the receding floodwater had left a dainty lace filigree, as delicate as spun glass and as easily broken. All my instincts were for silence, the better to listen and escape detection, but Ajax scrunched happily through it all, the proverbial bull in a china shop, while I was intent on skirting daintily round the Waterford crystal. The track grew rougher, the puddles deeper, and eventually even I abandoned any pretence at caution and tramped along.

The Bedford washes had been ice-bound for a week and the stagnant shallows were already frozen. Give it a few more days and we would be skating on them. However, the larger, deeper, and more sheltered sheets of floodwater remained open, the result partly of sunny middays and the action of great herds of mute and Bewick swans, the latter making the mornings charming with their matins of delicious hootings and cooings. Towards one of these large flashes I crept, cautious again, an Apache on the warpath. Ajax, catching my mood, slunk at heel. On this water duck would be resting before their morning flight to distant waters and other marshes, who could tell where?

We arrived at my favourite hide, a formidable oaken gatepost, its gate, the latest of many, long gone. The post leant at an angle which threatened to topple it into the dyke. Its head a tangle of rusty barbed wire into which the dead rushes, flotsam of the floods of a decade, had lodged; there was even an old blackbird's nest in it. There we settled down to wait on the trampled spot where I, and doubtless other fowlers, had lurked during many winters. Even in the quarter-light I could make out the flattened discoloured remains of old cartridge cases imprisoned in the ice.

Before us lay the water, a sheet of slaty black fringed with cruel ice. The dawn was close, the angry red slash across the east its harbinger – a wound which grew gangrenous with green and livid yellow and a purpureal black edge. With a noise like ripping paper, a spring of teal came from behind, made me start, almost took off my hat and landed with a dainty swish on the water ten yards away. Stone still for a cautious moment, they relaxed and swam hither and thither with clockwork movements. Ajax glared at them, himself a carved statue like those Egyptian dogs in old tombs. He glanced at me uncomprehending – how come I did not fire? Then with a *priiip* of alarm they were up, invisible against the paling sky and gone in an instant in the manner of their kind.

There was a gradual crescendo of duck noises in all directions as the light grew, and eagerly I peered this way and that. A herd of Bewicks flew over, hooting and calling like so many owls. They seemed black against the eastern sky and I could easily see how inexperienced gunners had been known to mistake them for geese. I watched them by, as steady as a constellation in line astern, messengers from the ice-fields of Siberia, and so no strangers to the cold.

The cold still air magnified the sounds about me and it seemed as if I were in the middle of a mighty concourse of wildfowl, but really they were miles away. Then some wigeon came, a great skirling army of them, lifting far off in a black cloud, gaining height and swirling

35

over me far too high to shoot. As they passed the line of the rim of the newborn sun, every white belly flashed a rosy pink and, whistling and growling, they faded from sight and sound behind me. More came and still more, seaming the navy-blue sky like a sewing machine run wild, in long wavy lines, echelons, chevrons, in all formations known and unknown to heraldry.

I could but grip the gun, impotent but longing, with the raw emotions and exposed nerves of adolescence, desperately wishing for a shot but also somehow frightened of firing in that magic place – it would have been akin to whistling in a cathedral. Mallard came, stuttering, staccato, altogether more burly than their smaller cousins, but, alas, either too high or too wide or both. In time resignation became apathy; it was almost full daylight. 'No shot for me today.' Slowly and stiffly I straightened myself from my half-kneel, half-crouch behind the post, commiserated with Ajax, who sat in gloomy unemployment at my side, and prepared for the long tramp back to the road. The gamebag flapped empty and mocking on my shoulders but I had seen things of which less fortunate men knew nothing and thus were the poorer for it.

Halfway back, head down, tramping grimly, I heard it – the magic, spine-chilling bugling of wild geese, rare birds on our marsh, although today they are more common. I gazed across the white-rimed reeds, shaded my eyes with mittened hand, and saw them, a skein of nine, flying in a line straight up the middle of the washes. My heart went out to them, for they were new birds to me, beyond my ken and the stuff of my wildfowling books and tall stories, creatures of imagination, things to dream of and no more, but surely not real. There they were, my very first sighting. How distant and unattainable they seemed!

Rooted to the spot, an earthbound beetle, I watched these glorious creatures. Would that some great power might divert them and send them over me! It has been a matter of eternal wonder ever since that, due to a never-to-be-forgotten miracle, that is exactly what they did. For no apparent reason they swung at a ninety-degree angle, lost height and headed straight towards me as though I myself had flown up and guided them. It was impossible – a dream, too good to be true. In real life such things just did not happen.

But it did, just this once. I hissed venomously at Ajax, who was snuffling about in the tussock. He sat, obedient for once, his near-white coat the perfect camouflage. I dropped to one knee behind a pathetic stunted willow bush; it was far too late to find a better place. On and on they came, my heart beating in time to those great pinions. Still they

36

called, a sound to make the blood run cold and yet boil it at the same time. Too late to plan exactly what to do; they were here. The moment was upon me.

Now with the calm of desperation, I heaved up the magnum, gave the leader a goodly swing and fired a single shot. In the time it took my heart to beat once I heard the pellets strike, a dry rattling *phruttt*. A miss, a miss! But no, the third bird in line was falling, suddenly shrunken and aimless, plummeting down, down like a stone to crash onto the frozen grass with complete, utter and exhilarating finality.

I fired no second shot, a characteristic I have since observed to be not uncommon with novice goose shooters. I bellowed to Ajax to 'Leave it!', for I did not want his hard mouth mauling my treasure. I ran to where it lay, eyes demurely closed in death, the beading of its blood startlingly red on the rime. Little as I knew of such things, I knew enough to recognize a whitefront when I saw one. Tenderly I picked it up and stroked its feathers; I would not sully that handsome plumage by stuffing it into the gamebag but carried it all the way to the old stack and then proudly home on my bike along the High Street for all to see how clever I was.

That was all of thirty years ago. The head of that venerable patriarch stares down at me from his plaque. There is a faintly censorious look in his beady, black eye. Ajax has long gone to the happy hunting grounds and I have since grown up.

But it was my very first goose.

CHAPTER VIII

The Shore Shooter

BONXIE

ROUND THE coasts of Britain, where the tidal rivers ebb and flow, on the miles of salt marshes that reach lonely and forsaken like a grey garland of autumn flowers floating in the tide, crouched by the winding creeks that crawl up into the land fed by sluicing tides, by forgotten little harbours of the south coast and the drowned lands where a sea-wall has been breached, and the hungry sea has swallowed back the land that has been won from it through the centuries by the puny ingenuity of man – there you will find him.

You will find him, too, in the damp gloaming of a winter evening; on the forsaken and wind-swept meal marshes and cockle strands of the Norfolk coast, where the east wind blows for half the year and the bones of wrecked ships strew the sandbanks and the great saddle-back gulls cry; where the white thunder of the surf forever forms a rhythmic backcloth of sound, and the seals bark on the long moonlight nights of autumn when the first of the wigeon rafts float into the eel-grass beds

38

on the flooding tides; on the bitter winter marshes of the Wash, where once the great fenland, unhampered and unchecked by the sea-walls, bred wildfowl that darkened the sky in their myriads and the spreading waters reached half across England; by all the sea-washed walls and gull-haunted marshes of our shores. Yes – there you will find him, the shore shooter, the man who finds his game below the level of the high-tide sea, between the marks of the highest tides and the lowest tides, on the sea marshes and the mud, and on the sand and shingle beside the sea.

His is one of the last of the old wild free sports. Not for him the coveys rising from the root fields in the hazy warm September morning, when the red admiral butterflies linger on the orchard wall and the hedgerow blackberries blush and darken in the sun. Not for him the stand by the spinney when the leaf is off and the pheasants curl over the tops of the beech trees as the tapping of beaters' sticks get closer. The roar and splutter of the tide and the wild chorus of the wildfowl are his requiem, if disaster should befall him by the treacherous sea, as it has come to many who made the mistake of staying too long and forgetting the tide. His is a lonely vigil, more often than not completely unrewarded in the material way of a shot at a duck, or perchance a goose.

He sees winter dawns like peach bloom over a grey sea, wild days of scudding clouds and thundering surf, nights of fitful moonlight and east winds full of wigeon voices. He seeks, on lazy, grey autumn days, the pools on the saltings where the sea asters are shedding their seeds and the teal may flight at dusk. (Teal love the seeds of the sea aster, and during the great teal migration months of September and October the aster beds of the coastal marshes are always worth flighting.) He sees the thousands of knots flying like a ragged scarf thrown in the sky, and the long lazy surf rolling up the beachways on that flat slobland of mud and sand far beyond the marsh heads at the foot of the low tide sea. Here the sea-bank looks like the far horizon and there is just the dim line of the land and the horizon of the sea and the world is of salt water and mud – a land that is neither land nor sea, but belongs to the fowl.

The genuine shore shooter is a lonely man, and he likes it that way. He shuns the company of his fellow men out on the marsh. His is the magic of the solitude, of the skyways and the tideways, and the redshank-haunted creeks. Of the lonely sheep walks and the samphire beds, and the marsh heads at full sea – those solitudes that can be shared only with a dog.

CHAPTER IX

—•◆•—

Tideline

SINBAD

TEN YEARS of age and dressed in a new, and smelling, yellow oilskin coat, with a sou'wester of similar colour stowed away in the dunnage lying at my feet on the planks of the jetty, I stood waiting for my father and the dinghy, which was at that moment shoving off from a little five-tonner that had just dropped anchor amongst the galaxy of other small craft lying a hundred yards out on the silver-grey water. This was to be the great adventure in which I was at last to spend a long weekend with my parent and his friend in the latter's little yacht, *Kestrel*. I had swaggered down from the boatsheds with what I hoped was a true nautical roll, and felt that I already looked the part to perfection. Seventy-two hours later a very seasick small boy was put ashore and was glad of it, but during those three days something irrevocable had happened to him.

Most of the time had been spent cruising in the sheltered waters of Poole Harbour, tacking painstakingly to and fro along its narrow

40

channels at low water, or running with keel up across the muds when the tide was at full. But it was at low water, when the acres of mud lay naked and exposed, that *it* had occurred; a love of the tideline, of the beauty and mystery of emptiness, of the wastes in which waders and wildfowl made their homes, had been born in me.

To many, such places are nothing but dreary desolation; to others maybe an attractive picture – in fine weather – if seen once in a while. But to the true fowler there is no place on earth quite like them. The silvery sheen of wet mud at sunrise; the hiss and chuckle of the tide as it seeps in or out, the piping of multitudes of birds, the unforgettable tang of mud and salt water, the warm glow of sunset – these are but some of the many moods of this hard and tough hunting ground. What of the others – of the bitter gales, the wavelets now turned to driving spume that whips and lashes the flesh with biting sting, the ice-rimmed creeks when the estuary is locked in the grip of arctic frost, the falling snow or deadly dangerous fog that can bemuse even the locals and cut them off at the mercy of the tide? There is no one to hear cries of distress. Wet, cold and desolate indeed, but what a place of enchantment and strange, gripping appeal!

Forty long years ago it entered into my blood and almost every detail of that first estuarine voyage remains clear, and the noises and smells of it, too, so indelibly were they impressed upon my youthful imagination. It was then that I first saw fowl as they should be seen, in masses and rafts, in skeins, and feeding naturally along the tide – mallard, wigeon, teal, knot, dunlin, shelduck, oystercatchers, 'shank, dotterel and others – and heard for the first time the magic call of the curlew. I have loved them all ever since. We laid up in a creek near Arne that first night, and two mallard and a teal were shot (it was in September and most holiday yachting was over). I stroked sadly their downy corpses, and almost wept over the beauty of the handsome teal drake.

The piping, burbling and whistling of waders, the lazy slap of water against the sides of the boat, the creak of timbers, the sough and moan of the wind in the rigging and, above all, the flat empty wastes – none of them was forgotten in that awful bout of *mal de mer* which overcame me as we beat round to Lulworth.

Came the time when, with a schoolmate as partner, an ancient and unsafe duck-punt was purchased for fifteen shillings, to be patched, caulked, tarred, and painted by our own inexperienced hands. Forays in Christchurch Harbour and forays into the reedbeds, where teal and an occasional duck were trophies indeed. More experienced outings in later years near Wareham and along the Solent, and then farther afield to the east coast. Ireland, and the first grey goose to crash down into a Wexford slob. The racing tides and rain-blurred estuary of the Humber; down to the Wash, shore shooting at first and then the delights – and tribulations – of a real gun-punt carrying a nine-foot breech-loading Holland & Holland. Over to the west, along the rugged coasts of Scotland, and countless unnamed and uncharted inlets and creeks.

A knowledge and understanding of tides, winds and flight lines, of sunsets and dawns, of flighting geese on the moon, standing knee-deep in the frozen bottom of some Norfolk or Lincolnshire dyke. The enthralling *whee-ou! whee-ou!* of wigeon whistling in under the storm-wracked moonlit clouds, or at the dark flight as winter's dusk gives way to night, and the murmur of the sea in the distance is a guessed-at background.

Of long hours dug in on a sandspit or mudbar, prisoned there until the ebb of the tide shall free one. Of breathtaking, sweat-making creek jumping, as one struggles across the marram grass and sea lavender of the saltings. Of a sudden total immersion in ice-cold water as a treacherous surface gives way. Of wet and weary hours in the punt, and probably nothing to show for them beyond a tingling exhilaration born of endeavour.

For some of us there is no form of sport to compare with it, but I think it must be bred in one. It is no armchair business, this coastal shooting; it is tough, lonely, and calls for extremes of endurance and patience, but if you are made that way, you are lucky. You have something not many possess, the entrée to a world few are privileged to know.

CHAPTER X

The Wigeon

HUGH FALKUS

MY FIRST shotgun was a present from Puggy Dimmond. He was an old man then and no longer went out into the misty sunrise. The gun was a double-barrelled, non-ejector, hammer 12-bore, made before the turn of the century and without any frills or fancy engraving. But it was strong and safe and beautifully kept; and still as tight as a rock when I used it last.

Puggy handed it to me on the saltings outside his boatshed one wintry afternoon, shaking his white head and spitting to cover his embarrassment as I stammered my thanks.

'I've a host of guns. I won't be using it again. Get out on the marshes wi' it and shoot some o' them owld ducks. You know where to go, you've been along o' me often enough.'

That gun became my proudest possession. Nothing I have ever owned, not even my first boat, meant quite so much to me. Pocket money was hoarded to buy cartridges, and the very first shot I ever

43

fired from it killed a pigeon, flying. A good shot, although I say it myself, and very encouraging. The subsequent discovery of a ring on the pigeon's leg was mortifying and gave Puggy much amusement, but, although a lesson in recognition never forgotten, did nothing to detract from the glory of the shot itself.

Every available moment of my winter holidays was spent on the marshes with that gun. Stalking along the tide's edge in Puggy's duck punt I shot my first curlew with it. I spent hours cleaning and oiling it. It hung above my bed. I dreamed of it on school playing fields, and many a ball whistled past into goal as I stood gazing at distant flocks of pigeon or plover, wishing myself at home among the lonely marshland fields and creeks.

In the winter, shooting was and always has been my life, and to me no shooting quite equals the pursuit of wildfowl on salt marshes. It has a strong, weird mystique which demands an affinity with loneliness, a love of solitude. Only the man content with his own company and in sympathy with wind and tide can really understand the fascination of wildfowling.

I have spent long hours on salting and sandbank under winter moons, and waited the daylight through in many a muddy pit and marshland hide; but of all the hours of daylight and darkness that hour of changing light at daybreak has always been the most exciting.

The day came when for the first time I went out alone on morning flight. It was a memorable adventure.

I dozed fitfully that night, constantly turning to glance at the loudly ticking alarm clock beside the bed, fearful in case I should oversleep. And when at last the strident ringing forced me into consciousness, I leaped up with a breathless anticipation touched with the magic which even now holds me in the small hours before an early flight.

I dressed with excited fingers, and swallowed the bacon sandwiches and coffee my mother had left out. Then, with Puggy's gun under my arm and a pocketful of cartridges, I hurried out into the cold, quiet morning.

The moon had set, but it was still dark when I arrived at the sea-wall. The fleet's black surface reflected the stars. An earlier cloud rack had drifted away and Sirius was flashing blue and brilliant in the western sky.

Frozen grass crackled underfoot as I scrambled up beside a rusty wire cattle fence which stretched from the fleet side to a stile on top of the sea-wall. A flock of mallard, alarmed by my sudden appearance on the skyline, rose quacking from nearby reeds, their wingbeats fading as they climbed away into the darkness towards the sea. In the estuary, far out beyond the saltings, winking fairway buoys and the red or green navigation lights of passing ships and barges shone with unusual clarity in the sharp still air.

Between sea-wall and estuary stretched the salt marshes, dark and mysterious and very quiet. Every sound seemed magnified by the frosty stillness: the rustling of a vole in fleetside rushes; a faint popping of mud, as the flood tide ran up the creeks and gurgled into innumerable little runnels.

Already there was a hint of daybreak. Cocks were crowing from distant farms. Somewhere a dog was barking. Soon the marshland sky would be alive with the rush and chorus of morning flight.

My sea-boots left barred footprints on the stile's rime-covered plank. I shone my flash lamp down the bank, slithered through the frozen litter of high-water line and squelched out onto the marshes. Gun on shoulder, I set off along the muddy winding track which led to the salting's end.

At a point where the thinning saltings joined a wide creek-mouth I jumped down into a deep, narrow gut. It was very cold, I laid the gun carefully on a clump of sea-blite, pulled up my jacket collar and buttoned it with numbed fingers.

Shorewards, somewhere among the saltings, a cock wigeon began to whistle. A loud, clear, liquid call, rising and falling like some high-pitched siren. Dark against the water's edge, a redshank dipped and bobbed, retreating with little spurts in front of the incoming tide. The stars were paling and the eastern sky had become suffused with streaks of light. Gradually, the creek's leaden surface changed from grey to silver.

Now I could see mussel and cockle shells in the mud, and the clear outline of my footprints. Tufts of sea-blite beside the gut took on a slight shade of colour. The sky had spread with lemon and the faintest pink.

Out on the estuary flats lines of curlew were moving back on fluttering wings, calling excitedly as the spreading sea swept them to higher ground. The redshank jumped from the creekside and flickered past me with a mournful shriek. As dawn light grew the marshes quickened into life and the air became full of sound.

A sibilance of wings. The wigeon were flighting. Fast-flying specks, glimpsed for an instant high overhead; the cock birds' whistle mixing with the hens' soft, rolling growl, as pack after pack flew with a sound of rushing wind towards the estuary and the sea. There, resting in long rafts far out among the waves, they would greet the sunrise.

With them came flocks of teal and mallard in tight wedges; a few shoveler and goldeneye and shelduck; and some pintail, silent among the noisy wigeon. From muddy creeks and reed-lined inland pools; from frost-tipped stubble, and fields where rotting potatoes lay half hidden; from shallow, crustacean-haunted salting flashes, and dark green zostera beds, they flew seawards high in the morning sky.

I crouched in the creekside gut and watched them pass by far out of range, the gun cradled in my arm unfired.

My hope of getting a shot had almost gone when three specks appeared low over the marsh coming straight towards me. I caught my breath in a moment of suspense. The specks, coming very fast, became duck-shaped. Another few seconds and they were above the creek.

Now...!

In my eagerness, I raised the gun a second too soon. The ducks, reacting instantly to this sudden movement, flared on loud wings. Even so, there was an easy chance; but as I swung with the climbing birds and fired I skidded on the slippery gut-side and my shot exploded into empty air.

By the time I had scrambled to my feet the duck were at extreme range. Aiming at the nearest bird I fired the second barrel – and instantly regretted it. The bird rocked and flew on for a short distance; then, with one wing tip splayed, it wobbled down on a long slant and splashed into the middle of the creek.

Leaning against the bank I suffered a flood of self-recrimination. After muffing the easiest of chances I had taken a shot which would have been far better left unfired. The result was a wounded bird, and small chance of my recovering it. By now, the tide was at a half-flood, the creek over two hundred yards wide and impossible to wade.

I stayed where I was, motionless. As Puggy Dimmond had taught me, a wounded duck will usually make for the nearest land. If I kept still and out of sight there was a chance the bird might swim to my side of the creek.

It was a cock wigeon. Its chestnut-coloured head with the characteristic light buff streak showed plainly above a grey and silver back. I watched it, wondering what it would do, which way it would swim. A light breeze had sprung up and was tending to push it farther out. Half rising from the water it flapped helplessly, its broken wing trailing. My hope dwindled. The wigeon stopped flapping and as though deciding on the easier route began to paddle towards the opposite bank.

Well, at least I could try to kill it outright. Pushing a cartridge into the choke barrel, I climbed from my hiding place and splashed down through the mud. Seeing me, the wigeon began to paddle faster, stretching its neck forward and swimming low in the water. I steadied myself at the tide's edge and fired. The shot, pitching at long range, kicked up an irregular pattern of spray harmlessly strung out and widespread. The bird swam steadily on.

I stared helplessly across the creek, the tide swirling round my legs. A flock of dunlin swept past flashing grey and white as they banked and turned together in perfect harmony. Overhead, herring gulls streamed shorewards and the air was loud with their crying. The sky was catching fire now. The faint early lines of lemon and pink had broadened to jagged bars of red and yellow flame. A mile away two figures moved along the sea-wall, black dots against a glowing sunrise.

The spring tide was flooding rapidly. Already it was gurgling into the footprints behind me, and lapping against the salting's edge as fingers of wind moved in quick darts across the surface. Surrounded by the rising water, part of the creek bank opposite had become an island.

The wigeon completed its swim. It climbed out of the water onto the far corner of the island and disappeared into a clump of sedge.

I knew what would happen to that bird. Rejected by the flock, it would remain a lonely outcast condemned to lingering starvation – until herring gull and black-back split open the wasted carcass and tore the heart out.

That a wounded creature should never be abandoned until every effort has been made to recover it is an inflexible shooting rule observed by every sportsman worth the name. This had been impressed on me since the earliest days, and I knew that the recovery of that wigeon, or at least its speedy death, was my responsibility. The bird's position was known. The difficulty lay in getting to it. Neither dog nor boat was available; the creek too deep to wade. What then? Had I made every possible effort? It seemed to me that I had not. For even if the creek could neither be walked nor rowed, it could be swum.

Standing on the thickest clump of marsh grass above the gut, I kicked off my thigh-boots and began to undress, setting the boots together on the wet ground and piling my clothes on top of them.

The rising wind was sharp on my flesh and instinctively I realized the necessity for speed. Cold reduced strength. The sooner the job was done, the better. Setting my teeth, I ran naked through the mud and plunged into the creek, gasping as the icy water rose above my chest. The bottom suddenly fell steeply away and I lunged forward out of my depth, swimming wildly, panting with every stroke for the clutch of the cold had made me breathless.

The current was very strong. No allowance had been made for drift, and before getting halfway across it occurred to me that my starting point should have been much farther upstream. Instead of turning back and starting again, I plunged impatiently on. Soon, a tiredness crept into my arms and legs. I turned on my back, snorting and spitting. The tide had already dragged me a hundred yards downstream of my starting point and in sudden fear of being carried past the island I began to flail away against the current in a frantic endeavour to regain lost ground.

Since that day I have swum icy creeks in many a winter's dawn. Experience taught me the correct technique and such a swim became commonplace. But this was the first time I had ever done it. It was also very nearly the last, for I was young and green and wasted my strength.

I was gasping for breath and pawing with weary arms when my toes felt the blessed touch of mud, velvety soft, and safe.

The current swirled round me, plucking at my legs; but using my arms like windmills I splashed up out of the creek and stumbled on to the hard ground by the salting tufts. I longed to pause and rest, but the wind was razor-edged now and, determined at all cost to keep moving, I forced myself into a run.

The wigeon took me completely by surprise. As I approached the clump of sedge into which it had disappeared, the bird suddenly broke cover and rushed towards the creek. Moving with astonishing speed, it avoided my outstretched fingers and flapped into the water. I plunged down the bank in pursuit and was about to grasp it by the head when, to my exasperation, it dived. It reappeared twenty yards farther out and began to swim quickly away along a creek at right angles to the one I had just crossed.

To give up at this stage was unthinkable. I was determined to catch that bird but, clearly, any attempt at swimming after it in deep water was doomed to failure. Some form of interception seemed the only chance. Keeping well away from the water's edge I ran through the mud parallel to the creek in which the bird was swimming.

A couple of hundred yards ahead I waded out along a shallow spit. There, crouched low in the water, its nose just above the surface, I watched the bird as it swam towards me. It paddled with urgent

48

strokes, glancing over its shoulder as though expecting danger from behind, the broken wing cocked upwards like a sail.

It came closer and closer, I braced myself to lunge...and then, inches outside my reach, the wigeon saw me and dived again. It surfaced a dozen yards behind me and swam steadily on with the current.

With a numbing sense of frustration and defeat I watched the bird swimming away down the creek. By now, my jaws were chattering uncontrollably and a strange lassitude was spreading over me. But I have never relished being beaten, and it was conceit, obstinacy rather than strength, which drove me on.

But wading out for a second time another two hundred yards downstream, I knew it would be the last chance.

This time, when the bird was still some yards away, I had a sudden inspiration and started to splash gently with outstretched hands. The wigeon hesitated then turned and slanted in towards the shore. Still splashing, I waded after it. It dived again, but by now the water was too shallow for escape and it began to swim in circles, flattened against the bottom. Then I fell on top of it and seized it by the neck.

I staggered back across the island to the main creek, which was swollen now and running very fast. My legs slid from under me and I fell in the mud. Remembering the two men who had been walking on the sea-wall, I looked for help towards the shore, but there was no sign of anyone. My pile of clothes on the distant bank looked small and far away; it did not seem possible that I could ever reach them. But the will to survive is very strong. I pushed myself up from the mud and stumbled into the water. It felt hot and sticky.

I swam on my back, and eventually the tide grounded me on a mud-spit. I crawled ashore on hands and knees. When at last I reached my clothes, I flopped on to them and lay there for a time, utterly exhausted. The dead wigeon was still clamped between my fingers. The skin below its throat had broken with the strength of my grasp and the mud plastered head stuck out grotesquely like a puppet's mask on a stiffened stalk of red neck.

CHAPTER XI

The Big Guns

ALAN SAVORY

EVER SINCE those who make our cartridge cases decided to give up manufacturing brass cases for 12-bore super magnums and 10-bores, and long-cased 8-bores, a great deal of the thrill of shore shooting has gone for me. I used to love the boom of a big gun at flight time. There was something almost primitive in these great heavy chunks of ordnance. You had to be strong to use them properly, but there was added adventure when fowling with a big gun. There were special goose guns that were used regularly on the North Norfolk coast; you could tell by the deep sound where they were. On foggy mornings, when the geese came in late from their nightly resting places on the high sands between Wells and Stiffkey, you could hear the deep boom of the 4-bores all the way down the coast to Blakeney and then the sharp double thud of the magnums.

There was never any slaughter of wild geese from these big guns, because they weighed so much that one had to be a giant to shoot with one with any degree of accuracy. There was one man I knew who used to shoot on the Breydon marshes with a double 4-bore weighing 22 lb. He was a huge man with shoulders like an ox. He once admitted to me that to get off a double shot at a party of duck was a bit of an effort: 'The old girl don't kick – she sort of pushes yer,' he told me, 'and yer gotter stand firm, or she'll ha' yer, bor!'

There was another mighty gun owned by a famous nose-and-throat specialist who used to shoot a lot at Wells. It was a 2-bore muzzle-loader with a hole in the stock so that it could be used as a punt-gun. The owner loved to load it up with a generous dose of black powder, a special felt wad and several ounces of BB and lend it to a friend and watch him get knocked off the sea-wall on to the road. He said it was one of the sights of Wells. All the fresh young guardsmen who stayed at Wells in the halcyon days of the grey geese used to eye the great gun with envy. And they all borrowed it – once.

The dawn would be streaking the eastern sky and there would be silent gunners all along the bank waiting for the goose flight. The huge gun would be loaded with great ceremony. It was a single-barrel with a welded ridge along the barrel which used to terrify me, as I always expected it to come apart. Then the goose-fever-ridden gunner would stand on the bank as straight as if he were on parade and loft the gun as soon as the first bunch of geese went over – never mind the height. There would be a flame like a sudden blowtorch, a deep boom, and a dense pall of smoke and the gunner would stagger back and fall into the road, to the wild delight of everyone. The new boys all had a go. No one ever told them! The gun was eventually given to me when the specialist left Norfolk, and now I believe is used as a small punt-gun, somewhere up on the Wash.

There used to be a lot of single 4-bores about on the coast in the days of the geese. They fired a charge of black powder in a green case and went off like a signal rocket. I saw a goose shot by one fall right out of the clouds like a hat falling out of an aeroplane. They were a useful gun in a sand-pit on the shore, but I never liked a single-barrel and they pushed one about too much.

Then there were the 8-bores – the brass-case 8s, and the ones that fired a paper case that was 4 ¼ inches in length. They weighed anything from 14 lb and were crippling to carry about. They did not kick like a long-case 12-bore, but it was advisable to stand with your knees bent so as to take the push. Sitting down in a hole in the mud or a hide amongst the shrubby sea-blite bushes was perfect for shooting with a big gun, as the recoil would sway you over in a controlled swing, and you could get your second shot off without staggering.

My own personal experience of the big guns started with the purchase of a magnum 12-bore brand spanking new at £12. It was a thoroughly good gun without any frills. It weighed 8 lb and had 30-inch barrels. It was my only gun for years and years and I shot all sorts of 'queer' cartridges through it – game cartridges, super magnum loads, home-loaded 3-inch cases full of Amberite powder and 1 ½ oz of BB, and 2 ½-inch cases with a bare ounce of shot and three drams of Smokeless Diamond for driven partridges. I shot game with it, until some bright member of the party got hold of it and made a scene about heavy guns and special loads. Then I bought a 6 ½-lb game gun and could not have hit a barn with it if I had been inside one and the door had been open, so I used to sneak out partridge driving with my old magnum and game cartridges and be told that I had recovered my form in some miraculous way.

However, the wildfowling bug had bitten deep and I got hold of a brass-cased super magnum 12-bore by Richard Jeffery Junior, which was a magnificent gun. You could clip mallard out of the sky ten yards farther than with the standard 12-bore magnum, but hasty loading from pockets filled with the thin brass crimped cases cut one's hands to pieces. Also, although the gun was very good with No. 3 shot, it would not handle BBs but crushed them up in the chokes. One of the Wells-next-the-Sea wildfowling guides took a fancy to it and we did a deal. I came out of the deal, which lasted for three days of argument, with an 8-bore with great hammers and an underlever action made by Cox of Southampton, a gun case, a cheque, and a biscuit-tin full of old black powder cartridges. Some of them were reloads and had candle grease melted in the tops instead of card overshot wads. It was a mighty gun and the first time I fired it on an inland marsh a great piece of burning paper came out with the smoke and set fire to the reeds. I had a grim half-hour beating out the flames. My shooting partner was so helpless with laughter that he was incapable of any assistance at all. But I loved the smoke and the 'boom-boom' and the adventure of the big gun. On the seashore, where the wind blows the sand like a moving carpet, it was the perfect weapon, with its underlever action and hammers, and never got clogged up. But the range was no more than a magnum 12-bore. There was just more shot on the target which meant that every bird hit was picked, which I think is the whole essence of wildfowling.

I had got the big gun fever badly by this time and toyed with the idea of swapping the 8-bore for another 8-bore which took 4 ¼-inch cartridges. I got one of the cartridges unbeknown to the guide and cut it open and found that the extra space in the case was filled with card wads, so that deal was off!

It is pitifully easy to make a huge bag of geese with an ordinary game gun if you know how to set about it, and there is nothing so disillusioning. All you need is the knowledge, a set of decoys and a goose feeding ground, and a moonlit night. It is a sickening performance, as I know to my cost. But to shoot wild grey geese on their flight lines to and fro on the saltings is a different thing altogether. There is something magical about it. The dawns and sunsets, the crawling tides, the winter gales and the great skeins of shouting birds riding the wild wind – they get you utterly bewitched, as do the roar of the great guns and the smoke.

CHAPTER XII

—◆◆◆—

Evening Flight

CMA

WHEN DOES the duck shooter become a wildfowler? That is one of those hypothetical questions which always seem to spring eternal, with its crop of argument and counterargument – the fowler so superior and scornful, in his tales of hardihood and endurance, the duck shooter with his counterclaim that an inland marsh can be just as wet, and by meteorological records a great deal colder. So they go on, finally to burn low and quiet, until someone throws in the billet of the old argument which starts up the sparks and flames once more.

I suppose the truth is that neither is right in that the question has no final answer, for no man chooses the worst weather, save for the fact that then his quarry is on the move, and, by stress of climatic conditions, likely to be more approachable.

One does, of course, make some virtue of necessity, and, 'full of strange oaths and bearded like a pard', expand in the bar parlour in contrast with those who have had enough sense to sit by the roaring

Mallard rising from Manor Farm meadows, Wretham, Norfolk   *Jonathan Yule*

Autumn Floods, Ouse Washes, Welney *Julian Novorol*

Teal over winter floods – Ouse Washes   *Julian Novorol*

The Moonlighters, Threave Castle   *Geoffrey Campbell-Black*

Brent geese over The Wade, Hamford Water *Julian Novorol*

Backwater, the River Dee, Kirkcudbrightshire   *Geoffrey Campbell-Black*

Wigeon in the shallows   *Julian Novorol*

Evening flight – mallard *John Paley*

fire. Both our types basically have in common a deep love of nature and an interest in more than the pursuit of a bird to kill it, for only by that can they ever survive for long the lonely vigils and light bags which so often accompany their chosen path. There must, too, be an appreciation of nature in all her moods, not only in her soft and yielding moments in September, but also in her hard, aloof hours under the winter moon.

I looked back at an old diary of a September day, and the few figures brought back all the details of that day. It had been hot and tiring as only a September day can be and consisted of walking up the coveys of partridges in the time-honoured fashion of the country, until every swede and mangold seemed the size of a coal scuttle, and the energy required to surmount them became more and more, while one's physical resources became less and less. We walked out the last patch of roots at about 5.30 p.m., and collected to count the bag – ten and a half brace of birds, a couple of pigeon, and a hare which young Dick had shot first thing, and which he had been told to so-and-so well carry himself; he looked as if he had had a bellyful of it too!

The more elderly and the less keen departed, and the four enthusiasts who wished to wait for the duck flight into the Wet Field adjourned to the Red Lion for ale, bread and cheese. We tramped into the low bar with the hobnails rattling on the quarried floor, ducking our heads under the low lintel. In the window hung a pot from which trailed a campanula in a cascade of white blossom. The pub was as yet empty, for the village was still occupied in washing up the milk things in the dairies, or getting out those few rows of potatoes, so that our host had time to spare to settle down and discuss the day's sport, with which, being country-bred, half-farmer, half-publican, he is well conversant.

The dogs, punished heavily by the heat of the day, stretched themselves luxuriously on the floor licking a paw, or busying themselves with the removal of a briar or thorn, until the torment of nettle stings drove them to jump up and rub their feet vigorously on the quarries.

The first pint slipped down rapidly, and, with the fatigue of the day, and on empty stomachs, soon released the tongues whose strings had been tightened since mid-afternoon. With the bread and cheese and second pint, strength flowed back once more and plans were made for the evening. One or two of the locals dropped in and mentioned the duck which had been seen heading in at dusk, so that their quacks and chatter sounded like a veritable farmyard. These rosy pictures led the less experienced to buy drinks which stimulated the teller into even more extravagant stories, together with old-time anecdotes which brought in old So-and-so's gun. Every village has one, usually single-barrelled, and the story of its deeds makes one realize how the art of barrel boring or cartridge loading must have been lost!

The window was small and the light in the room began to fail, and, fearing to be late a start was made for the rendezvous. Of course, one was really far too early, but we hurried the half-mile or so, only to be half an hour too soon. Still, that was of little consequence as one sat in the cool mellowness watching the creatures of the day settle down to slumber while the nocturnal ones emerged, for nature's shifts work by the sun, and as the light fades one packs up and the night shift comes on.

Wet Field consisted of a shallow sheet of water, some two hundred yards each way, bounded on the north side by a ditch lined with willows, and on the west by a large patch of sedge and reed. The south side comes up to a hillock covered with alder, beyond which is a field of stubble. This pool is filled to capacity by the snows of winter, but during the summer the level falls until there is some twenty yards of glyceria and marsh grass which very often goes well awash again with the August rains, and this forms an ideal feeding ground for duck. Shoveler in particular seem to love this spot.

I sat with the young retriever bitch on a batten of straw dropped amongst the sedges, while just in front lay a tangle of bulrush and reed-mace which appeared to be the roost of all the swallows in the district, for the birds jostled and rustled amongst the stems as they settled for the night. Occasionally a bird rose, and swooped and hawked over the reedbed and gathered a few bedtime morsels from the insects which abound, and which made their presence felt upon my neck and wrists. A drowsy twitter spread over all, until a new crescendo rose, as one of the late feeders disturbed the rest as he elbowed his way into the ranks.

A water-vole, lulled into a feeling of security by our immobility, advanced along a rush stem near my feet, and on it he suddenly decided to feed. His sharp chisel teeth cut through the rough leaf edge with a noise that seemed momentarily deafening in its suddenness. The dog rose with paw raised to investigate the intrusion, but a hiss made her sit once more, but with rigid posture and raised ears. The vole plopped into the water and vanished for good.

The sun had by now vanished from sight, and only showed its presence in the rays which cast a ruddy margin on the lower side of a strip of stratus cloud low in the western sky. The willows on the far side showed only as black outlines, which cast an equivalent patch of darkness across the water now showing like a bowl of silver. It was warmer, after the warm day, than the usual cool evening air, and the mist rose like wool in patches across its surface.

An old owl hunts the reedbed regularly, and he suddenly appeared at eye level as noiseless as a ghost. We were simultaneously aware of each other and he swept aside silently, while I swung the gun barrels up in a reflex over which I had no control. There was a harsh rushing whirr and a very soft thud, followed by two more – snipe! I stood motionless and all was silent, until I moved my position in order to face the remaining light. This alarmed the snipe and with a harsh *scaap* they flew away unseen. It was then that the bitch stiffened and looked upwards. I heard no wings, but the trilling double whistle of teal circling the pool. There came a shattering report from the far side which sent snipe complaining in all directions, and four mallard suddenly swept in to me, and I dropped two which smacked into the marsh. I sent the bitch in immediately, for a winged duck in this morass is a match for any dog, if given time to recover from the shock of the first impact.

More shots rang out, followed by a lull; then in the fading light there was a splash on the pool and a heavy *kronk* betraying shoveler. But they distrusted the deserted appearance of the pool and rose over me and I got the drake, but missed the duck. That was the end and after a while a whistle was given, and we slowly moved out of our stands to meet in the lane.

The pages of the diary turn and a new picture of the Wet Field is recalled. My companions were reduced to one – two if Susan is included. The willows now swept up with bare wands, which rattled in the gales, while their dusky companions, the alders, showed gnarled limbs and twigs knobbly, with the cones so beloved of redpolls, which disport themselves more like tits than finches in the pale winter sunshine.

There was much more water now, and in places only the tips of the sedges showed over the surface. The swallows were now catching their insects under an African sun, and the reeds which were their sleeping quarters were dry and sere, so that the breeze no longer whispered through them as they swayed, but rattled and hissed through their oft-broken stems. Yet, though stark and harsh, the old charm was still there, perhaps even enhanced, as the bitter hop may give piquancy and satisfaction to the ale.

Susan was older and wiser in the ways of her trade than she had been in September, and the remainder of that September party had decided that harsh winter breezes were less attractive. My companion and I had been busy all day ferreting out the rabbits from the banks, where their presence will jeopardize the young wheat, the green blades of which are already strong in the field. We had munched our sandwiches behind the hollies while the 'felties' *chak-chaked* as they flew over the fields in disorderly flocks and at three o'clock we had packed up, and, loaded with rabbits, boxes and grafting tools, had retraced our steps to the farm.

A quick wash and a cup of tea in the wide kitchen with its hearthful of slumbering cats, and we had been ready for evening flight. The lights had already been shining from cow-house doors through which came the rhythmic click of the milking machines, so different from the lantern and hand-milking of the old days. We had still been too early at the marsh, but had filled in the time by moving some faggots to make a dry stand, on which was placed a sack to protect Susan from the rheumatism which so often is the lot of the water-dog. The greyness thickened and the pool was harsh and silent, but old brown owl was still there, and we gave each other the same start. It seemed as if the flight would never begin for these birds had learned wisdom in the hard school, and there would be none of this easy sailing in, in comparatively good light. Many would be wigeon, and they would flight only when it was practically dark.

The teal came in first, and they got clean into the water without a shot – a hiss of wings, a splash, and they were down. The other gun spoke, and the birds skimmed past like flying bottles against the sky – a miss with the right barrel, but the same bird down with the left. Then far away the ringing whistle of a cock wigeon. I whistled in reply, and a paltry imitation it sounded by comparison, but it sufficed. There was immediate answer and in they came, without circling – a steady fall on fluttering wing. I fired and shot over, but caught my bird as it rose steeply away. A splash on the water, and then two shots from the other side, with two more splashes to spell success. Susan was at my side with the white shoulders of the bird showing in the gloom. The next wave of wigeon followed, and we got another three between us. Then the flight ceased abruptly and we began to wend our way home.

The stars showed brightly – sure sign that shooting light had gone. We passed the cowsheds again, now silent save for the cough of one of the herd. Now we had reached the car, and another flight lay behind us.

CHAPTER XIII

Much Fouling on the Marsh

BILL POWELL

T HERE WAS no doubt about it, our 'goosing' holiday looked like being a bit of a fiasco. For some years Jack, Tom, Bob and I had joined forces for a glorious week on the marshes after wild geese, and this year we had struck a spell of 'butterfly' weather the whole week. What made it the more exasperating was the fact that there were thousands of geese coming off the flats every morning and returning there on evening flight many gunshots high and all we could do was to stand and watch them with clean barrels.

The moon had been full at midweek, and we had a tried a couple of night shoots with similar lack of success. As the tide streamed in over the mudflats the clamorous hordes of geese walked in before it, sometimes taking short flights but never coming into the marshes. When they approached nearly within shot they would take to the glass-like water and swim around just out of range.

By Friday morning Jack and I were gooseless, while Bob and Tom had only one apiece – fine greylags, both singleton birds which had given the only real chances during the whole week. I saw Tom get his bird, a nice shot, cleanly killed, but Bob was by himself when he got his.

True wildfowlers learn to take things as they come, but it must be confessed that that cheery *bonhomie* that characterizes wildfowling parties was not so much in evidence that Friday morning as we sat around the wreckage of the breakfast table.

'The glass is as high as ever, and rock steady,' complained Tom. 'Looks as if we've about had it this trip.'

'P-p-plenty of t-time yet,' replied Bob the optimist, whose stutter became more pronounced when he was weary – and we had all had a gruelling week. 'T-tell you what! I'll b-bet you a b-b-bottle of Scotch I take more geese home than you do, Tom.'

'You're on,' said Tom, ever ready for a bit of a gamble. 'We're level pegging at the moment. If we tie, we each buy half a bottle to celebrate our success or drown our sorrows.'

After breakfast Jack, Tom and I set off to the town to buy peace-offerings for our wives. Soon after completing our purchases we were having a pint or so in the town when Tom had an idea.

'I'm going to pull a fast one on old Bob and buy a couple of geese from the poultry shop if they have any,' he told us, and laughed in anticipation of Bob's discomfiture.

'Oh, I say,' protested Jack 'That's a bit low isn't it? You can't take Bob's whisky off him that way.'

'Nonsense,' Tom replied. 'What Bob said was "I bet you a bottle of Scotch *I take back more geese than you*." Nothing was said about shooting 'em.'

After some discussion Jack and I agreed not to spill the beans and we set off for the poultry shop.

'I've just got two wild geese left,' the shopkeeper said. 'They are very scarce at the moment, and I sold a couple a few minutes ago.'

A sudden suspicion flashed across my mind.

'Tell me,' I said. 'Was the chap who bought them tall and thin, with a dark moustache?'

'That's the chap,' he replied. 'He had a bit of a stutter.'

My suspicions were confirmed, and I roared with laughter. Not so Tom.

'The double-crossing hound!' he spluttered, and turning to the shopkeeper urged, 'Look here, You *must* find me a third goose.'

'Sorry, sir. The locals are not bringing them in this mild weather. I've no idea where you could get hold of another.'

'That makes it still a draw,' grumbled Tom on the way home. 'I never suspected that old Bob could be so crafty.'

Which remark, let's face it, had its funny side!

Evening flight came and went, and though three or four wigeon were bagged the geese flew out as high as ever. After supper Bob said in rather an offhand manner that he was going to have a last look round the marshes by night and prepared to set off. We announced that we might go out later, but it depended on what the sky was like. At the moment conditions looked pretty hopeless – not a cloud to diffuse the moonlight, and not a breath of wind.

About nine o'clock we turned out to have a final look at the weather, and if conditions have ever been more hopeless for a wildfowling expedition I hope that I never see them.

'I vote we go round to the pub for a snifter and turn in early. I feel I could do with a good night's sleep,' said Tom. 'I'll pretend I've been out and shot these geese. Old Bob will never know, and it's a million to one against him getting another.'

Things did seem hopeless, and so we agreed on this course.

'Glad you've come in, sir,' the landlord greeted me. 'You've won a prize in our Christmas draw.'

And with a broad grin on his face he produced from behind the bar – a wild goose!

For a moment silence reigned. Then the full humour of the situation struck us, and a shout of laughter went up. Here were we, comfortably ensconced before a roaring fire, supping ale, and a goose was thrust upon us, while poor old Bob was toiling over the marshes without any real prospect of getting a shot.

'I'll give you ten bob for that bird,' said Tom eagerly.

'Nothing doing,' I replied, 'I got this by fair means which is more than you can say about those two you acquired in town this morning.'

'I'll make it a quid,' he persisted.

Now I can use a quid as well as the next man, and a goose that I had not myself shot held no real attraction.

'I'll toss you two quid or nothing,' I countered, for Tom was well blessed with this world's goods, and I could see that he was determined to have Bob's bottle of Scotch, cost what it may.

Luck was with me, and Tom cheerfully handed over a couple of pound notes in exchange for my prize.

'That makes me four against Bob's three,' he chortled.

None of us heard Bob return that night, but when we all rallied in the gunroom before flight the next morning he produced his two geese in triumph.

'I'm going to enjoy your bottle of whisky, Tom,' he gloated.

'Hey! Not so fast, me lad,' replied Tom, producing his three geese from his game bag. 'Had a bit of luck last night,' he prevaricated. 'Got a couple out of a little bunch of four, and then got another singleton later on.' Which up to a point was true!

Bob's face was a study as he set off alone for morning flight.

We never got a shot that morning, and on the walk in Tom kept chuckling away to himself about something. I asked him what the joke was.

'I've set up two decoy geese at the far end of the muddy creek opposite the quay,' he explained. 'Bob is bound to spot them with his glasses after breakfast, and it will be a scream to watch him wallowing up the creek after them.'

Bob had a habit of walking down to the quay after breakfast to survey the marshes, and true to form he duly turned out on this Saturday morning. We watched him return with studied nonchalance and hurry into the gunroom to pull on his waders before any of us spotted those 'geese'.

When he was safely in the creek we all stood on the quay watching him creep through the mire, nearly bursting ourselves with laughter. At length we estimated he must be getting almost within range of the decoys and were preparing for the dénouement, when to Jack's and my delight and to Tom's horror five greylags appeared with wings set, about to drop in to the decoys.

Bang! Bang! went Bob's gun, and down plummeted a beautiful right-and-left, which were duly collected, together with the decoys.

'Bit of luck someone leaving those decoys out there,' Bob said with a grin on his return. 'But for them I should have lost that bet. I'm going to enjoy your bottle of Scotch, Tom, old boy!'

62

CHAPTER XIV

Wildfowling in a Storm
DUGALD MACINTYRE

I T HAD been hard frost with deep snow on the ground for more than
a fortnight, and with the thaw had come a heavy fall of snow in the
night. With the dawn the wind had veered from south to west, and a gale
had sprung up, which increased in violence as the light grew stronger,
lifting the water from the pools of rainwater in the fields in great sheets
of spray. Storm-lashed cattle, drenched and miserable, found what shelter they could behind partly submerged hedges, while the roar of the
surf on the not far distant beach sounded amid the roaring of the gale
like the bass *profundo* of some majestic concert.

Such a day is the delight of a hardy wildfowler. Duck are hungry on the
first day of a thaw, and, in the wild west of Scotland, they flight inland in
daytime to the flooded fields as the storm rises and the sea becomes too
rough for them to sleep on in comfort.

A country so flat that the river running through it spread for miles over
the fields was the scene of our hurricane shoot, and the multitudes of

63

duck seeking shelter in the lee of the long lines of partly submerged hedges were worth coming far to see. On the widest swamped area swam possibly a thousand mallard, and in the next field as many wigeon kept up a whistling concert. Three or four hundred teal wheeled endlessly at one part where tall rushes showed their tips above the water, and, as we looked, we saw a flight of magnificent pintail come in from the Atlantic with the storm.

Fresh arrivals from the sea were greeted by the duck already on the water with a chorus of quackings, whistles and grunting calls. Now and then a discontented mallard gave vent to her feelings in a loud burst of quacking.

There goes a gaggle of quite a hundred greylags against the storm. They are forced to make long tacks just like ships and, at one time half a mile distant from us, at their next tack's turning point they are almost upon us. Eleven great whooper swans come over a distant plantation, and their anxious leader thankfully finds an alighting place on the ruffled water, across which sweep intensifying blackening gusts. The worst of those gusts lifts the water into the air in solid sheets, and the duck swim closer to the sunken hedges.

There was room and to spare for a dozen Guns to hide between those duck and the Atlantic when one of us went round the submerged country to fire a shot and so put some of the duck over his companion. It had fallen to my lot to be the ambushed gunner, but it was difficult to find any cover on the line which the duck must take for the sea. I crept along at the root of a half-submerged hedge for some distance towards the likely flight line, and was finally stopped by an open gateway. To cut a few hedge branches occupied no great time, and I took no notice of duck passing within easy range, as to shoot at them meant putting off the main body of the duck flotilla in the wrong direction.

Two distant shots from my companion, and the duck began to flight to the sea over the open water. Flight after flight passed out two hundred yards from my station. As my companion came nearer to the line where I waited flights of duck began to pass almost within shot, but, as an old wildfowler, I refused to be tempted into firing wild shots. I had my reward at last, for a fat mallard duck, rising in front of my friend, was passing out to sea at a fair range when she dropped. I had six of her companions down in the next few minutes. When my friend arrived I found he had two mallard, so we had not done so badly, and we had lunch in the lee of the hedge before making for home (as we believed) with all the haste possible, as what had been a storm rapidly became a hurricane.

As we cowered in our scant shelter the duck which had flown out to sea found it rough and back they came to the inland sea, flying faster down the wind than I have ever seen duck fly. We separated to take advantage of the opportunity of a lifetime, and I saw my companion, who was a really great Shot, get a number of mallard in quick succession. I was kept busy myself until I had an accident. A big flight of wigeon had just one fat mallard drake in the middle of it, and I kept my oncoming shot for him. The duck were coming so fast that neither of us could have more than one shot at each flight. That shot had to be taken at that point in front when oncoming birds are flying on practically the same level for some yards. The drake was fairly hit, but he had his revenge. His forward impetus made him hit the water of the muddy ditch in front of me like a shell. I had both my eyes wide open, and the result was that I was out of action for some time.

My friend had seen what happened and he gave up his shooting and rendered assistance in mopping up operations.

It was time to make for home indeed, for as we pressed against the hurricane we had difficulty in breathing, and made scant progress. Our route for home was through the long golf course which there borders the sea, and at the height of the storm, which coincided with high tide on this rare occasion, we saw the sand-cliffs which border the sea melting like butter at each impact of a victorious billow. Those tall sand-cliffs were normally a long way from the sea, but that wild evening old Neptune broke all bounds and the whole contour of the coastline was altered in the few minutes when the tide was at its highest and the hurricane at its worst.

Four miles to walk in that hurricane was something to remember, and each of us had at least a dozen mallard to carry.

As we left the coast and began to pass near the storm-lashed farmsteadings, we saw that the straw from blown-away ricks littered the fields. As we passed one of the biggest farmsteadings perhaps half a mile distant, we saw the entire heavily timbered and tarred roof of a sixty-yard long straw shed up-ending and trundling across country, levelling all fences in its route until it came to rest in the heather.

That was the greatest storm I was ever out in, but what a splendid show of duck round the lamplit kitchen floor when we reached home!

CHAPTER XV

Flight of a Lifetime

BB

THE HEN-WIVES of Stainmore Forest were putting their charges to bed as we crossed the Pennines. Over the darkling fells white troops of ducks waddled towards their respective farms, and beyond Kaber Fell a monstrous black cloud, shaped like a giant's head thrown backwards, was shutting out the last of the light.

Mac, Charles and I were on our way north, all of us hunting the grey geese in autumn for the first time. We had wearied of the oft-repeated assurances of the crofters that November was the best month for the geese. Many were the tales we had heard of loch-side pastures grey with pinks; of how November was the great meeting month of all the brave armies from over the polar seas.

So now this was it; we were on our way, nearing the completion of the first lap of our long journey. I sensed the same old carefree happiness. Ten days of freedom lay before us and the sombre fells – incomparably rich in colour, madders, golds and tawny-lion-tinted grass – were dimming in the November twilight adding to this sense of new adventure.

There was the little inn beside the Esk where we stopped the night and dined regally for the last time in civilization. A fine old burgundy, shrimp cocktail, and roast pheasants, the roaring fire and talk of fishing days with the rod up that delightful river in summers long ago.

Next morning it was on again through Eskdale with the beech woods a riot of unbelievable colour, a feast for any artist's eye.

We arrived the following day at our destination and instead of going straight to our HQ we made a tour of the goose country which lies next the firth. I was on tenterhooks as to what we should see, and the glasses were out every half-mile scanning the rich green pastures below the mountains. It was a very rough evening with a rising storm; indeed, it was the beginnings of one of the wildest, wettest nights in the highlands of Scotland for many a day, though we did not know it then.

We scanned all the old well-loved haunts in vain; not a goose did we see. This was very disturbing, and I wondered whether all those accounts we had heard of the grey legions had been mere fairy tales.

With the fading light we made for the coast, and just at flight time Mac spotted the first skein passing in about a mile distant. The time was about 4 p.m. We got out of the shooting van and for the first time felt the buffet of the wind. It was so strong that we sought the shelter of two peat-stacks at the end of a bank, and in the lee of these we watched a dramatic scene.

Out on the firth a tawny tide was flooding full. White horses leapt and roared, crashing one upon the other in a tumult of foam, and as the scene darkened there began one of the biggest flights I have ever seen – certainly the biggest evening flight of grey geese. We decided afterwards that they must have been new arrivals, for they came from a northerly direction, dropping down over the mountains. They came in low, gunshot high, and had it not been for the 'Sawbath' we should have got the guns out of the van. Yet I was content enough to watch and not to shoot, for I sensed the drama of the moment.

The skeins came battling in, line upon line. Those that were close at hand never altered course as they neared the peat-stacks behind which we crouched; they battled low over us, hardly making headway, huge black wings looming darkly in the twilight.

We looked along the coast in the fading autumn dusk and as far as we could see other skeins came battling in, mere dusky lines and clots; the stream was never-ending. I suppose over two thousand geese came in that night, and they were still coming when it was too dark to see. The tumult of the storm whipped away the wild crying of their voices; we only caught snatches of it now and then. With the geese came fieldfares. They, like the geese, were fighting the wind; they, too, dived down to the shelter of the rough heather on the shore.

Back in our HQ that night we wondered if the storm would hold. The weather forecast was reassuring: 'Gales round all our coasts.' We heard of lifeboats being out. Outside the wind was roaring and raving, and driving sleet rattled on the windows.

The next dawn, the Monday, was perhaps the wildest day I have ever been out in. It was with difficulty that one could stand up against the wind and sleet. Before the first glimmer showed in the east we were in our old places, Charles at Smith's Post, Mac at the Goose's Graveyard, myself at Leaning Buoy – all places well known to us from previous years.

The tide was washing the 'brews', a smother of dirty foam. There was no mistake about it, this was the hour, this was the place. The tide was right, weather right, and the firth crammed with geese.

Early, very early, before it was barely light, the geese began to move. They came in small parties from all sides, whisked by the wind, hurtling like blown rags. It was not easy shooting. I missed again and yet again. Not only geese came by me from all angles, but mallard – scores of mallard which kept passing shoulder high. Never was there such a flight!

Though Charles was not more than two hundred yards or so to my right, I never heard him shooting, but time and again I caught faintly on the wind the boom of Mac's great 'mountain gun', as we call his big double-8.

Fieldfares rose up from the reeds all round me, plover were tossed about, more duck and more geese! When all was over and light had come over the savage scene, eleven geese were down and gathered – six to Charles, two to Mac, and three to me.

It had been one of those mornings which happen but once or twice in a fowler's lifetime. Had we shot better, our bag would have been doubled, but that did not worry me: wholesale slaughter is distasteful to the sportsman.

Other good flights were to follow during the ensuing days. One morning, with the help of another sudden gale which arose at flight time and died at midday, we even managed almost to equal the previous bag, but not one of those occasions could ever match our first morning. I shall not forget it as long as I live.

CHAPTER XVI

Under a Waning Moon

MICHAEL SHEPHARD

T HE GROWING moon and the full moon usually produce nights when the birds move erratically and the flight is long drawn out. Also, the light is often very bad for shooting. If you are to wait through a bitter winter's evening on a bleak marsh and then on through the night, just waiting for the arrival of birds which may come in at all hours, you must indeed be keen and hardy.

But the waning moon offers a rather different set of conditions and – such a night having produced one of the best flights I have known – I think it is worthwhile to consider just the sort of things that may happen.

The occasion I have in mind was one of frost – another frosty night after ten days of prolonged frost. The moon was due to rise at 8.30 p.m. and was four days into its third quarter. The place was a narrow marsh through which runs a small stream; the stream, swollen as a result of the daily thaws, had managed to keep open a patch of water about two acres in extent and for a week I had been feeding that place.

We had intended to shoot earlier in the week, but one thing and another kept us away from that particular marsh. In fact, I doubt whether we should have gone at all had it not been for the local information that several flights of geese had come up river soon after moonrise on the previous evening. This called for a recce of the valley and our investigations revealed a fair few signs of geese and a great many of duck on the Starveal Meadow. That was why we decided to venture into the frost after an early supper.

Now, as we have agreed, moonlight produces a rather prolonged sort of flight and also encourages the birds to wander about after their initial feeding far more than they do on dark nights. But once there comes a certain period of real darkness between dusk and the moonrise the birds come in at dusk, or with the moon, and this really produces two concentrated flights instead of one rather problematical long period during which the duck may arrive at any and all times.

When the wigeon and geese have started coming into the valley, we have flighted teal and mallard at dusk, retired for revival once the initial flight was over, to return in time for the rise of the moon and the arrival of the wigeon and whitefronts.

As we approached the marsh soon after eight o'clock, we agreed that it was milder, but that it would freeze again before midnight. Parties of mallard kept springing up and winging their way unseen above us as we waded through the dabble to set up our decoys. Usually, we shoot the different marshes so infrequently that a steady flight has been established and decoys are not necessary for an ordinary dusk flight, but under the moon some duck fly about in search of pastures new. They investigate barren water warily, but come confidently where good decoys are used.

We hoped to get some shots at those birds which we had disturbed (they would not be long in returning to the good food they had been forced to leave), at duck coming in for their initial feed (those which had waited at rest for the moon to rise), at mallard wandering on reconnaissance after feeding elsewhere for two or three hours, at wigeon arriving from the distant estuary and, perhaps, at a skein of geese in search of food or fresh water. Some mallard were already circling the flood again as (having set the decoys and dumped a lot of poor potatoes) we worked our way to the shelter of the hedge for a final cigarette. There was as yet no shooting light.

After a while, John said, 'The wind's veered.' It had, round to the south-west, which reminded us both of the persistent weather forecast that 'rain will spread from the south-west later in the day'. In fact, when

70

the moon lifted over the Cotswolds we saw that it was rising behind a light screen of spreading cloud. The light changed most subtly and it suddenly dawned on us that it was indeed light enough to shoot by when a single duck jumped from its feeding place on the water quite close to us and was clearly seen both against the moonpath on the water and against the sky. How it had come in unheard, I do not know, but duck do these things.

Conditions could scarcely have been better for us as we separated: the wind was stiffening from the south-west – the direction from which most of the fowl would come – and this would force them to circle and make their approach against the lightest part of the clouds. From my place against the dark line of the hedge the decoys stood out clearly in the dabble, shifting positions slightly with the breeze. Then, above them, there appeared a shape which was lost among them as the splash of its landing came to me. That duck must have made a long, gliding approach, for I had heard no sound of its wings.

However, it sat out there and quacked loudly for a couple of minutes until there came across the marsh that low guggle which betrays mallard coming in to feed. As I saw them appear and grow against the shining backcloth of the clouds, I realized that there were duck everywhere over the marsh and saw another bunch of nine birds turning over the far bank. They came back quickly and low, almost in line, but just as I was about to fire my bird jinked and they all climbed after the report of John's gun broke the night. By the time I had got on to my bird again it was too late, but I heard my companion splashing out to pick up his.

'It's a wigeon,' he called, and sure enough, from way down river, down by the town, there came that lovely whistling and we knew that others were coming to us. Before they arrived, however, two mallard gave me a perfect chance, but I dropped only one and left the second to fall to John's gun as it climbed straight over him.

There was no time to pick up; the wigeon were with us and came in with none of the usual caution they display. In fact, for the next twenty minutes there was no question of going out to get our duck. Mallard, wigeon and teal (we did not shoot at them) kept coming to the decoys and to the food which lay beneath them. Two wounded birds were shot on the water and lay there, drifting with the wind. Immediately, five mallard swept down to pitch beside the bodies and left another floating there.

For some while it was quite surprising that both mallard and wigeon chose to join the inert bodies of their fellows. We picked up four mallard, five wigeon and a shoveler from that place, while our score from the area of the decoys – some twenty-five yards away – was three mallard, a wigeon, and another shoveler.

The lull came suddenly after half an hour. It was our opportunity to clear the field for further action, although it might have been better to leave the birds where they were since they seemed to work as well as the artificial decoys. I can only think that they simulated feeding birds and that the light was not clear enough to betray the fact that several were lying belly upwards.

As we were collecting the last of the fallen, the cry of a pack of whitefronts sent us back to the hedge. The geese made no bones about it; they flew straight in, whiffled round sharply and pitched on the ice about seventy yards below us, never offering a chance. Very quietly I moved up to John and we slipped through the hedge, to creep back along it until we were near the geese.

There were eight or nine of them about forty yards away, but the light at the bottom of the marsh was not really good enough to show them clearly; elm trees obscured most of the moonlit area of the clouds and a deep shadow seemed to lurk about that corner, throwing the rest of the open marsh into an almost daytime brightness. I wanted to get closer to the birds, but once through the hedge even a belly-crawl from the shadow of the hedge would be betrayed by the cracking of the ice.

Finally, John moved farther down to a point over which the geese ought to fly when I put them up into the wind. Then I crept through the hedge. Before I even began the crawl I froze at the sound of more geese and soon saw them dimly as in a line of some thirty or forty they just cleared the willow trees beyond my friend. I waited for the shot and the birds were almost by me, thirty yards away, when it came, John told me later that they were so close above him that he had to wait before he could shoot.

The bird nearest to me staggered and then fell to the second barrel, forcing me to swing on to another and then in front of it. That fell, too, but my second shot was checked by the appearance of great shapes flying steadily at me – the nine originals had taken off into the wind towards John, had turned at his second shot and, without climbing, were cutting over the hedge within ten yards of where I stood. By the time I had pulled myself together and swung round on to them, they were but ghosts fading into the bad light against the background of the hills. I fired rather wildly, but hit a bird and then cursed the empty case in my other barrel. A shot came from the corner and as its echo faded round the valley there was a heavy bump far up on the ploughing.

While John went off in search of that bird I picked up his first one and mine. That was it. We could have waited on and we would have had more shooting, for next morning the signs on the grass and in the dabble told a tale of both geese and duck. Feathers and droppings were everywhere that was open; the potatoes were nibbled and most of the other food was gone. The springer brought me another wigeon which was lying dead on the ice, but which bird, or whose bird it was, I do not know.

However, I do know that it was just about as perfect a combination of conditions as we are ever likely to meet in the valley – hard weather which reduces the area of potential feeding grounds and brings a concentration of birds to those which are available; a good light to shoot by and a wind which turned the duck arriving out of the darkness; an area which could be fairly well covered by two guns (four *might* have been better); natural cover which did not perturb the birds and which allowed us to fire from close range and produced only two wounded and none lost. Finally, the knowledge that, after we had gone, the fowl returned and found the food they needed so badly. Everything conspired to produce an evening of really good, clean sport under a waning moon and we can reasonably expect to repeat the experience at some future date.

CHAPTER XVII

A Right-and-Left

BB

IT WAS good to be back again, very good indeed. As usual, nothing was changed – the stackyard where we left the shooting-van, the familiar light burning in the farmhouse window, the tramp across the dark, frozen fields which bordered the marshes. As always, we stood awhile listening for the first sounds of the geese, a sound last heard twelve months before. In addition to my regular fowling companion, Mac, I had with me Tom Nott, a newcomer to the game, who had never shot a goose.

My companions went off into the darkness and I made for my favourite gutter, which I knew I should find unaltered. I know this coast as well as my own garden at home; even in the darkness I could jump hidden creeks into which a stranger would have fallen headlong. By the time I had settled down, dawn was coming up over the hills on the far side of the estuary. It was a windless, cold morning.

As it grew lighter I saw for the first time the white frost on the grass. Out on the water I heard the *quink wink* of the pink battalions, as well as the sonorous *quank ank* of greys. Some of the latter had gone off from the marsh edge as I had made my way out. To the east hills grew plain. A golden flush tinged with pink brightened every moment. It was not the sort of morning on which to shoot geese – no wind whatever, a clear sky. Surely they would come in high.

The gulls began to flight in, redshank tripped along the muds where a flooding tide was filming the flats until the gutter a hundred yards off began to spill over like a full glass. Amazing how quickly the flats are awash. The shallow flashes in the muds, the runnels and feeders fill first, then they suddenly spill over until what was satiny mud is creeping, crawling water as far as one can see. Geese moved up the tide, swinging in two miles above me – pinks without a doubt. The greys had moved far out and sat cranking and gaggling on the water.

I was well down in my gutter, sitting on my goose-bag. I was so well screened I could sit as in an armchair with my eyes just on a level with the herbage – an ideal ambush. Quite suddenly, I heard close by a low cackling. Instinct made me flatten on the mud parapet in front. At the same time, my finger slid the safety catch forward. A party of about ten greylags were coming bang at me along the edge of the marsh. It was an easy shot. They came straight and low, appearing huge in the early light. I waited until I knew I had them well in to me and stood up quietly and swung on the leading bird. There was no mistake, no hurried, excited poking. I pressed the trigger as the magnum 12 was swinging and when it had blotted out the leading bird. The goose fell like a lump of lead within thirty yards of me. The second barrel was a miss, as it so often is with low geese.

Could I find that bird? No, sir! I searched and searched. I knew it was stone dead; I knew it lay within a few yards of my ambush, but everywhere the creeks wound about, a foot wide and three deep, fringed with marsh-grass. I had to call up Tom, who had a splendid little spaniel dog. Though other geese were moving, I wanted to make sure of my bird. This is sound reasoning – always get your goose if it is down. For ten minutes we searched and the little dog plattered up and down the hidden gutters without result.

All at once, I found I was looking directly at it. It was at my feet, right at the bottom of a deep, narrow gutter. I picked it out and shouted to Tom. At the same moment, I saw another bunch of greys coming in rather high from the sea. We both dropped in our tracks. They came right over in a V. It was a perfect chance for a right-and-left, as long as one kept cool and did not hurry. I remembered lessons learnt by watching the Duke of

75

Bedford's head keeper at some field trials at Woburn a few weeks before. No hurry, smooth swing, confidence, an excitement suppressed! Bang! Thump! Bang! Thump! One goose fell almost on top of Tom; another fell twenty yards away in the longer stuff to be retrieved by the spaniel. Tom's shot told also and another goose fell on the left of mine, but in thicker cover. This last bird we never found. It must have got away down one of the deep creeks.

By now the sun was shining brightly and the flight seemed to be over. But yet another skein hove in sight – this time, pinks. They were high. Again they came over, and at my shot the leader staggered and set its wings. Down it came in a shallow dive to disappear over the edge of the sea-wall. We walked straight over. Out on the plough was my pink, a strong runner, which the spaniel quickly brought to hand.

So ended what was a most satisfactory little flight, though I should like to have found Tom's goose. He was to shoot his first bird a few hours later, and several more before the trip was over.

A few days later, Tom's dog made a wonderful retrieve of a goose which he had shot out of a big skein and which fell far out near the tide-line, across a deep, unwadable gutter. It was a pleasure to see the little dog getting closer to that far-off motionless lump well out on the muds where no human could go. It carried it right back to the barn without once putting it down, and swam over to us as proud as Punch. Dog work is always a delight to watch – it adds so much to the joys of fowling.

CHAPTER XVIII

Fowling on the Ronds

ALAN SAVORY

I T WAS in 1933 that I first shot on the ronds. Rond is the East Anglian name given to the reedy banks of the rivers and estuaries between the water and marsh-wall. They are reed-roots and land liable to flooding, and the name is derived from the Saxon or Norse. Usually, they are just the narrow margins of reedlands beside the river, but sometimes they bulge out and are of considerable extent. These particular ronds were large and were beside the River Waveney, on the Suffolk shore, just past the Burgh Castle yacht station by the top of Breydon Water. There were several large tidal pools in these ronds which completely dried out at low tide to leave semi-saline mudflats. Snipe and other waders that came to them were in amazing numbers, and it was a favourite place for ruffs on migration and a great spot for greenshank.

Lying right in the flight line between Breydon and Fritton Decoy, that once-upon-a-time great arm of the sea that thundered on the sandy shores of the Herringfleet hills a thousand-odd years ago, and now lies tranquil, deep and shingle-bottomed, probably the finest pike lake in England, surrounded by trees and heathy pinewoods in the heart of the Somerleyton estate, the ronds were a good duck shoot. There was always a chance of a shot at flight, whereas farther along the river bank one just missed the flight line. Early in the season it was a great place for teal and shoveler dropping in to feed on the thousands of tiny shrimps and sandhoppers that live in the brackish water of the little pools. It was a tiny piece of the old wild fenland.

I shot on the ronds with Captain Aldridge, who then lived in Great Yarmouth, and had the shooting after the first fortnight of the season. It was a pleasant place of reeds and windmills and far horizons, and salt tides surging up the River Waveney, but after the home bred duck had left there was not a lot of fowl using the place, as the natural food supply sought deeper waters after the first frost, and the duck went elsewhere to feed. Even so, there was always a chance of a shot or two at high-flighting fowl on their journey from Breydon and the sea to Fritton Decoy. In rough weather, the pools, being salty, did not freeze easily, and fowl came to them in quantities.

During December 1933 it blew a wind-frost from the east, and the broads were frozen overnight and fowl flocked in to every sheltered piece of open water. They came pouring in to England with the freezing gale in their tails from the Baltic and the great marshes of Europe – small, dark mallard from the thirty thousand lakes of Finland and the cold ice-blue meres of Denmark. Norfolk became full of wildfowl while the easterly blow continued. I shot a brent miles inland while duck flighting on a far broadland marsh, and there were smew and scaup in the River Yare. It blew a freezing gale straight off the Steppes of Siberia from 1 December for seven days, without break or a let-up of any sort, then on 8 December it eased a trifle and the wind swung round to the north; it still froze up at night, but the days were milder.

All this time the night flighting on the tidal pools in the ronds was good. All the fowl were these little dark foreign mallard. Then, on 18 December, it started to thaw and there was no wind at all. We got just two mallard that night on the big mudflat in the ronds, but there was a continual winnowing of wings from far up in the darkening sky, and there right up against the stars were pack after pack of duck off to their European winter home where there were miles of thawing flood and acres of quiet meres and secret lakes, and we knew that for the time being, at any rate, the cold weather had gone.

About this season I had managed to get hold of a brass-case ham-merless 12-bore – a lovely gun. It weighed 10 ¼ lb and shot 11 ¾ oz of No. 4 shot perfectly. I shot duck right out of the clouds with it, almost twenty yards farther than with my old paper-case magnum, but I never could get it to handle big shot like BB as well as it shot No. 4s. It seemed to blow the middle out of the pattern.

I liked that gun a lot, I had a good afternoon on the coast with it and shot a brent and several wigeon one stormy day, but there were some unaccountable misses with big shot at geese, which was upsetting, to say the least. Then one January morning after a night of westerly gales and driving rain I went out in a flaring red windy dawn on to the Acle Marshes for the goose flight. There was a waning moon at six o'clock in the morning and the geese should have been in some time, but they were still out on Scroby Sands. Aldridge and I crouched in a dyke over our knees in water right up till eight o'clock before we saw the first lot like a wisp of smoke over Yarmouth town. They had a hard job to fly against the wind and veered all over the place. There were lots of geese, all in little scattered bunches struggling against the wind with a background of madly turning windmills and a red- and orange-streaked sky. It should have been a perfect goose-shooting morning for both of us, but Aldridge broke the recoil pad on his 8-bore and was finished for the morning after the first shot. I had a bunch of geese right over me, almost standing still, and just managed to wing one, and to kill another with one pellet of AA in the head. A most disgusting exhibition! And that was the bag for the most perfect morning for geese that I have ever seen.

My last shot of the season was in February. There was a 26-foot tide at 5.15 in the afternoon on the North Norfolk coast, and somewhere in the Blakeney district Drake and I sat in a hole in the shingle amongst shrubby sea-blite bushes, waiting for whatever flighted with the tide. It was almost a flat clam. The tide rolled in in long rollers which just managed to turn over on the shore. Several brent and wigeon sat far out on the sea. There were a few large flocks of knot away towards Stiffkey, and a few waders paddling at the edge of the sleepy tide. A woodpigeon came wearily in from the sea and from high up there was a sudden noise like tearing paper and a peregrine appeared like a falling stone. The pigeon dropped almost to sea level, the falcon just touched it, and it fell in the tide, where it floated a hundred and fifty yards away. The falcon zoomed up just in time to save itself following the pigeon into the sea, and swung like a black star over its prey. Then all the godwits in the area flew round and round and mobbed the peregrine, until it shot away inland, leaving the pigeon drifting in with the tide.

Peace then returned to the shore. A seal, riding the long oily swells of full sea, came and looked at us and stayed for some time before going farther up the harbour. The pigeon came to life and took off from the lip of a wave, and just made the saltings with staggering flight. We almost gave it a cheer. The sun dyed the west a deep orange and purple; clouds floated in the east in an apple-green sky. A few shelduck flighted down the harbour, to join the straggling lines of distant wigeon and brent.

CHAPTER XIX

One Morning Flight

BB

WHAT ARE the first birds to move on morning flight? This, of course, varies from coast to coast but I have noticed that it is rarely the geese; indeed, geese are usually the last to leave the sea for their feeding grounds inland.

Let us for a moment visit a Scottish firth I know very well, and which I have seen under all conditions – in frosty hard weather, in driving snow, and on those calm, mild mornings we so often get on the western seaboard. Let us take for example one of these 'open' mornings in early January.

There has been the usual procedure so well known to fowlers, the shrill of the alarm clock, the reluctant rising from bed (and it is amazing how the body complains at having to rouse itself at 5.30 a.m. on a winter's morning), the quick gulp of hot tea and a sandwich, and the journey to the shore. All this takes place in darkness, for on this morning we have chosen there is no moon. It is at such periods that the flight is most sustained. When the moon is full, wildfowl feed largely at night.

We have groped our way over the fields, we have reached the sea-wall and before us, showing as an indistinct blur, is the open sea and the dark tones of the marsh. We know the route well, even on so dark a morning, and are not trapped by that hidden gutter, or the soft spot which is so beloved by snipe. Actually, we disturb one as we pass this little bog, though it is, of course, invisible. It gives one *scaap* and we hear the 'prutt' of its spring into the air.

As always on the coast, there is a wind, though this will die at dawn. Twenty minutes creek-jumping and we reach our favourite place, an angle of the creek where the mud forms a seat. In front there is a low parapet, exactly like a trench in that other war which is now only dimly remembered.

There is no sound of geese, not a croak not a call – no sound at all save the far-off murmur of the tide.

Slowly the light grows over the sea, and then strange dusky shapes appear out of the dimness. They may be flotsam of the tideline, they may be tussocks, they may be geese – the eye strains to make them out.

A curlew calls far away over the flats; you can hear it passing down the tide, its voice growing fainter. These are ever-restless birds, even on the darkest night.

There is always this wait, but how enjoyable it is! Never a dull moment! The dog beside you, crouched low in the crab-grass, has his head up, staring out towards the sea. He hears and smells things you are not aware of; his frame quivers against you, for he is excited. A comfort, too, on a cold morning; a dog is a hot-water bottle as well as a retriever of his master's game.

Now the sea is visible, a spear of brightness, and yet the dark mysterious lumps are still unrecognizable. Funny how easy it is to imagine that they are moving! If you look at them long enough you can swear they take the forms of geese, and you can even see their spindly necks and small, wise heads.

Whistling wings pass over, not from the sea but from the land. A big party of duck has passed directly over you, but you could not see them, though the dog did. He stares up and takes a sidelong glance at you, which is very amusing. After the duck there comes another party. You saw those for an instant and they were in range. The gun twitches on the arm and is couched again; no gunner in all the world could have taken so fleeting a shot.

A goose calls far off, another answers, and then there comes the thin keening of gulls, a cold thin-drawn sound which always seems to me to have something of the desolation of the vast seas in it. And then the first birds come. They are gulls, a small party, wagging their way inland in a compact bunch as orderly as geese. Silently they pass. Soon after come others, until wherever you look gulls are coming in. Then a bunch of curlew. These, unlike the gulls who came silently, call to one another – clear yodelling cries, sounds beloved of the fowler. Their wings are working at twice the pace of the gulls'.

Those dark lumps out there are tussocks: at least you think so. They have not moved. Your imagination has played another trick. A redshank appears suddenly, sees you and gives a *twee* of alarm. Immediately afterwards a mallard plumps down on the wet sand not thirty yards off. This so often happens at morning flight. No doubt he has been feeding inland and has stopped for a snack before passing on to the sea. The spaniel's ears nearly fall off, and you whisper to him to keep down. But before you can begin to lift the gun the mallard has seen you and is up. By the time the gun is at the shoulder, he is away.

All this has taken a second or two. When you next look at the 'tussocks' your heart gives a bound. They are not tussocks, but sleeping geese! They sit all along the fringe of the marsh edge, strung out like beads on a string. Every bird has its head tucked in, but you can do nothing about it. They look just in range, which means they are over a hundred yards away, and even as you look one pulls out its head and stands up. These geese have no doubt but lately come in, and are off their guard. One by one they wake up. They are still silent; geese resting on the marsh edge are often as quiet as mice.

Now the birds begin to waddle slowly away. They sway, or rather roll, as they walk, like sailors – a true nautical gait. It is difficult to judge distance and movement on the open ooze. For a moment you cannot tell whether they are going away from you or walking in, but you know it cannot be the latter, as geese never walk inshore at dawn. Every bird – there must be thirty or more in front of you – is swaying but they are dwindling in size.

Then, with a clamour and a threshing of wings, all are up. No, they didn't see you. They are eager for a wash and brush-up in the fresh burn water which flows in over the muds half a mile from shore. The whole line swings right-handed, and you see them land again, far out on the burn edge, where they begin to splash and cackle and chase each other. Not until the sun peeps over the mountains and the whole firth is visible in the clear pellucid light do the geese start to think about breakfast.

There are fully three hundred pinks and greys far out on the sandbanks, arranged in a black ribbon. One end of the ribbon lifts and the ripple passes like a snake along the length. A moment's pause and the full glorious music crashes out as though at the bidding of a conductor's baton. Now as you look, to left, to right, the limpid dawn sky is spotted with weaving bunches all passing inland. What a moment that is! If you see no drama in this, then you are no fowler.

Most parties are low when they cross the muds, but they are climbing all the time, and as they cross the gullies they are out of gunshot. Some fool along the coast has two barrels. You see a skein lift and a moment later hear the shots – a tiny double pop. One big V comes straight for your ambush. Out of range. Don't be a fool. Yet the urge to fire is almost irresistible as with wry neck you look upwards under the rim of your hat. Clear in the light they pass right over, each stern snowy white with paddles neatly tucked, necks moving, all cackling. Some writers call it 'honking'. No goose honks save the Canada goose which makes a noise like a deep-toned cowbell.

We might as well face it, we are not going to get a shot this morning. We need wind, the answer to the fowler's prayer, to keep them down.

And then happens one of those quite unforeseen happenings which add so much to the uncertain joys of fowling. The sun well up, and the flight over, we are tramping back across the marsh, thinking of breakfast, as hungry as those old grey-bellies which are now lowing on some distant pasture. There is a single croak behind us. We swing round, dropping by instinct to one knee. And there, almost on us, is a party of six greys intent on committing suicide. Why this sometimes happens I have no idea, unless the geese are watching that other shore-popper who is making his painful, stumbling way to shore half a mile to our left.

The gun goes up, the geese scatter at the movement, each bird climbing desperately, silently, not even calling, so intent are they on gaining height. Bang, and again bang! The long cases of BB shot whistle skywards. The cackling breaks out and you cannot believe your eyes when no goose drops. Are these birds wearing armoured waistcoats? You've bungled a good chance.

Unbelieving, sick with anger and disappointment, you stand like a heron there on the saltings, fingers automatically reloading. You watch them reform and go on steadily shorewards. They are over the sea-wall now. Quite suddenly, without any fuss or warning, you see a goose slump from the middle of the skein. One moment it was flying as well as the others; now it is falling like a black rag to earth. Fortune has relented at the last moment; you have a goose down after all.

You arrive at the bank in record time, with your spaniel bounding in front. You range the sea-wall frantically, straining to catch a glimpse of an inert grey form. But the wind stirs the grass, other geese pass in unheeded (they are still moving in), a hare sits up in the middle of a green field washing its paws. You rake the pastures with your glasses. Farm carts move towards steaming middens, fieldfares cluck overhead, all the bustle of the day has begun. The spaniel ranges along the foot of the sea-wall his feather wagging urgently. Did that goose drop this side of the bank or over the land? How difficult it is to tell from the marsh!

Then comes the supreme moment. The dog pauses and casts quickly. He stops half-hidden by the rushes; his head is down, there is a pause, then he raises it – and, yes! There in his mouth is a bulky grey form, limp, with wings drooped awry.

'Good old fellow, good old chap, bring him on, bring him on!' Is there any prize so much worth while as this massive grey bird, warm to the touch, with hanging pink paddles and stern as white as sea foam?

There is a point in this account which is worth remembering. Always watch the skeins after you have fired, follow them out of sight. One single BB shot may have gone home without your knowledge, and many a bird is lost in this way. The pattern of BB at long range is fairly open; it is often the single pellet which brings down a bird.

CHAPTER XX

---◆◆◆---

Fowling Days

ALAN SAVORY

THE YEAR about which I write was an extremely wet one in these parts. In fact, so wet was it in the early summer that there was a great deal of floodwater lying on the marshes, and a surprising number of duck about when the season opened. There was one evening in the warm gloaming of September that is a very pleasant memory. I had settled down for flight in a sitting position on my side-bag stuffed with dry grass on a little knoll amidst an acre of so of shallow floodwater lying on the surface of a vast expanse of feeding marshes which stretched from the uplands to the sea in a great sweep of green and brown and blue distance. The water was not more than two or three inches deep, except where cattle had splodged across it. It was stagnant, too, as it had lain there all the summer, and most of the grass had gone brown. There had been a thunderstorm the night before, which had freshened it up, but there was no real reason why duck should use this particular flood, as they had so much other water to choose from.

Greylags leaving Loch Eye   Geoffrey Campbell-Black

Teal at Funton Marsh, Medway   *Ian Phipps*

Mallard early in the day *Geoffrey Campbell-Black*

Brent geese at sunset *Julian Novorol*

Winter wings – teal   *John Paley*

Pintails low and fast   *Geoffrey Campbell-Black*

The gnats were bad and there were columns of them floating in the sky like smoke. There was no bird life of any sort for at least half an hour. Some colts in an adjoining marsh were apparently holding a private rodeo, and kept thundering down the dyke wall to the marsh-gate overlooking my marsh, and then, after snorting a few personal remarks, thundering back again, manes flying with great clods of mud thrown from their hooves landing in the flood.

After a while, seemingly from nowhere, three stints and a reeve, obviously on migration, suddenly appeared amongst the short grass standing up out of the floodwater and began chasing insects. They chased about right up to my knoll, and then I spoilt the party by firing at a teal and missing it as it suddenly streaked overhead. There was no real sunset, because of the heavy thunder clouds. It just got gloomier and gloomier. Once there was a whicker of mallard wings far overhead, and the distant quacking of a duck. Once a hoarse croak from a flying bittern sounded far away where the river lay lost and reed-fringed in the sultry dusk.

When it got quite dark there were many little voices far away up in the sky, seemingly right against the stars. They seemed to be those of migrating golden plover and godwits, and once or twice there was the tittering cry of the whimbrel. There were several little parties of peewits which were camping on the marsh, and, just before it was too dark to see, one or two snipe flew over, but far away. From a shooting point of view the flight was a complete washout, but very enjoyable all the same.

A wet summer was followed by a wet autumn, but there was no east wind and the weather remained mild and muggy. After the homebred duck had drifted southward there were few migrants to take their place. There was a bomb-hole on the marsh not far from a bend of the river where I often stood for flight. It was on a marsh off my boundary, so there was nothing much I could do about flighting it, but there were a few mallard using it just before it got too dark to shoot, and once or twice, when the wind veered them a bit, they came over my bend of the river. It was a lonely spot – completely flat marsh intersected by dykes with nothing to break the horizon but the distant trees of the uplands across the valley, and a drainage mill here and there following the bends of the river. When daylight faded into dusk even these landmarks were invisible, and there was nothing but the water noises of the river and the sighing of the evening wind in the reeds. It was not a good place for flight and I got only one or two duck in the many times I went there, until one cold afternoon late in December.

I had no intention of going flighting, but word had been sent to me by a marshman friend that there were some geese using the level. These were the first geese to have been seen in any numbers that year. When I arrived at my spot in the bend of the river I saw the geese. There were about two hundred of them, and there seemed to be about as many whitefronts as there were pinkfooted. They were very wary and restless; five whitefronts flew down the river quite low, but saw me hiding in the reeds and went back and put up the rest of the geese. They all went up the river far out of shot and left the marsh lonely and forsaken. There was no bird life, but a seagull or two drifting over from time to time, and as the afternoon drew on the wind freshened from the sea and moaned bleakly over the marsh. I had an eight-month-old labrador puppy with me, and we sat together by an old gatepost watching and listening for the faintest sign of wildfowl.

It turned very cold at flight time, and it seemed as if there might be a frost later on. Then two mallard flew over the river wall in the very last of the sunset glow, and I missed the one in front, but got the drake. The flight was made. I had got a mallard, the pup was as pleased as me, and I decided to stay until it got completely dark, in case there was a chance of the geese coming back. We waited there in the cold until the stars were visible, and it was all but pitch-dark. We were just about to start on our long walk home along the river wall when the geese started returning down the river. They came in little lots and none of them was high. They were just visible now and then against the loom of the stars, but they all and every one were wide and out of shot of our stand. They came each side of us time after time, but just too far off and we never got a shot.

The noise they made, wild geese calling in the night sky, was more than thrilling, and we stayed by our gatepost till the last of them had passed over and their voices had died away.

The marshman said that as I had not shot at them they would most likely use the same levels for a day or so, and that it would be worth while coming again. It disturbs geese just as much to shoot at them out of range as it does actually to shoot one. If people would only realize this, and hold their fire until a really good chance presented itself well within range, there would be fewer geese peppered and fewer disappointed wildfowlers.

The next afternoon the wind was in the same quarter, but the sky was clearer, and there had been a sharp frost. We took our lonely stand by the same gatepost. I did this because the geese had come over each side of me the night before and there was no reason why this should happen twice, and if it did not happen twice they would come directly over my stand – unless they decided to fly the other side of the river. There was no sign of the birds at all, and the great stretch of marshes was completely empty of bird life the entire afternoon. I sat on my side-bag with the puppy labrador sitting bored beside me.

Geese are always a little unsettled when they first come to fresh marshes, and this lot were new to the neighbourhood. They take several days to form regular habits of flighting. We sat out the half-hour of daylight without hearing or seeing a sign of a goose, or anything else. The only sound was the bitter sighing of the reeds as the wind swept in from the sea across the lonely miles of drained cattle-feeding marshes. Flight time came at last, but tonight there was no sudden whicker of mallards' wings; no snipe called and tore earthwards in a sudden rush of sound; no green plover made plaintive music on the wind. There was nothing, not even a jeer from a passing seagull.

Daylight faded into dusk and the grey day became darker until the stars came out as the clouds cleared from the sky. I put two BBs in the magnum in place of the No. 7s and No. 4s which I was using for duck. Hardly had I done so when from right overhead, about forty yards up, came the sudden call of geese. I could see their black shapes against the stars and the sky, which had not quite assumed that inky blackness which makes flighting birds quite invisible. There were four of them, and at the shot one came plummeting down into the reedbed by the river, and the puppy went over the marsh wall into the reedbed after it. They had vanished in the dark before I could get a second shot, but there were more following, and the night became suddenly full of goose voices.

The noise was terrific, almost deafening. The pup came back onto the wall without the goose, just as I shot at another lot passing over nearer to the river. I saw a bird fall then more went right over me, and at these I had no time to shoot. One could hear them, the beating of their wings, and see a sudden black shape against the stars for a second or so – and then they were gone. There was a lull in the flight, and I thought it was over and went to help the dog with the two geese. He had found them in the reeds, but they had gone through the frozen crust of cat-ice left by the ebbing tide, and were too heavy for him to lift. Both of them were stone dead.

While we were getting the second one, another lot of geese went over, a bit farther out this time, nearer the river. For a moment they were just visible against the faint afterglow of the western horizon. At the shot one crashed into the river with a splash that almost shook the marsh. I stopped the puppy going after it, although he badly wanted to. An ebbing tide on a dark night is not the place for puppies, goose or no goose. Next day we found it stuck in the reeds a few yards out. It was a whitefront. The other two were pinkfeet.

I shot nothing else from that place that winter. The geese were back to their regular habits of bygone seasons within a day or so – resting on the sandbanks at night time and feeding on the fresh marshes by day. Every morning they came in at full daylight, flying high and straight to their grazing marshes up the valley, and every evening before the last of the light had gone they were up and away out to sea and the banks by the running tide. It takes rough weather and storm and snow to unsettle them once their habits are formed. You must get them when you can – and you do not get many chances.

CHAPTER XXI

Duck Shooting at Sea

SEA-PIE

A LARGE picture called 'Black-Duck Shooting at Sea', by the late Frank Southgate, of Wells, in Norfolk, hangs above me as I write. It was done in the early years of the century and is one of the best pictures that fine artist ever painted, the birds appearing almost to move and to be alive. Black-duck shooting was a popular sport in days gone by. It began to decline after the First World War, and is not greatly indulged in at the present time, owing to increasing expense of the boats, two of which were required with a couple of strong and willing rowers in each. Besides, sportsmen today shoot only edible wildfowl.

A day's shooting at sea was sport we once looked forward to, and it often happened that a few wigeon or the odd brent would be added to the bag. One boat was anchored and its occupants put out a string of roughly shaped wooden decoys – in fact, black bottles bobbing in line together were nearly as effective – while the second boat rowed round Holkham Bay and put up the birds, for which the simplest decoys seem to have a fatal fascination. I believe that the professionals at certain places where 'hard fowl' are abundant are reviving it. I shrewdly suspect that black duck form one ingredient, together with gulls and starlings, in some of the potted meat which finds its way into the sandwiches with which I am occasionally regaled when travelling.

In about 1910 I was beginning to make the collection of wildfowl now in the University Museum at Cambridge. Many species can only be obtained at sea, and occasionally I had memorable sport in pursuit of duck, divers, and grebes, and other seagoing fowl which were not then protected by law.

I had many good days at sea off Walton-on-the-Naze on the Essex coast. This was more accessible to London for a Fleet Street clerk than the Norfolk harbours, and I became acquainted with two brothers who often took me to sea in a shooting-yacht with an enormous stanchion-gun in the bows. This form of shooting is the *crème de la crème* of wild-fowling. There is a thrill about 'sailing onto' fowl which is only shared by the punt-gunner, with the additional luxury of a half-deck cabin whence to watch and follow the movements of the birds.

I hope even the most youthful sportsman is well acquainted with Folkard's *Wildfowler*. If he will turn to the steel engraving entitled 'A Scientific Shot at Brent Geese' he will find shooting from a sailing yacht depicted under ideal conditions – a rippling but not rough sea, with flurries of snow to hide the yacht from the already anxious fowl.

When I first went shooting with the Walton brothers I observed with admiration mingled with awe the skill with which one would manœuvre the yacht, sailing 'wide' of the fowl, and then, at a word, 'bring up' suddenly to the restless quarry. The stanchion gun was allowed a recoil of a mere couple of inches. The brother taking the shot would move the long barrel a trifle to left or right, and then lie across the breech, and, keeping his eye on the fowl, pull the lanyard.

It looked quite easy, but when I tried my prentice hand I managed to get behind the weapon instead of above it, and – well, it did not quite break my shoulder. After that I always kept a long way back, which was quite the wrong way to shoot, according to my expert mentors. I never had enough practice to become an adept at the sport, but enjoyed scanning the water for flocks of fowl, or desirable specimens, and generally returned to London early on the Monday morning with a nice bunch of fowl, and perhaps some 'good bird' which found its way to Rowland Ward's shop in Piccadilly.

A great advantage of sea shooting is that fowl can be followed about anywhere, if the skipper is well acquainted with his locality. But I have a vivid recollection of one occasion when a large and tempting flock of brent pitched on some awkward muds in Harwich harbour just awash with a falling tide. The skipper thought we had 'just enough water' to sail onto them, But we hadn't. It was the only miscalculation which I ever remember him making, and we neatly slipped the yacht into soft mud at the moment when we were congratulating ourselves that 'ten or a dozen' were practically in the bag. I can assure the reader that if one *must* be stuck on a mudbank for a tide a shooting-yacht has advantages which a gunning-punt does not possess.

To turn to a very different form of shooting at sea, some of the most enjoyable days I ever spent have been when rock (rock dove) shooting amid splendid scenery in some of the wilder districts of Ireland and Scotland. A large, roomy boat allowing complete freedom of movement is essential for this sport, and if two men are to shoot from it they should be well experienced in the handling of their weapons.

If a youngster is taken rock-pigeon shooting he should be the only one in the boat to shoot, for the excitement of the chase, and the motion of the boat, necessitate particular care in the use of a gun.

A year or two ago, when living in Caithness, I was anxious to get a few specimens of the wild rock dove where the breed is found in all its purity. As our boat approached the great cliffs between Dunbeath and Latheron, the scene became very animated. The ledges were crammed with shags, razorbills, and puffins whose cries mingled with the thunder of the green waves beating on the red rocks. At such times it is impossible for the human voice to be heard, and this is a factor which renders extra care desirable in the presence of a gunner without previous experience of sea shooting.

It is essential to shoot very quickly at rock pigeon; at least that has been my own rule, which has given satisfactory results. The birds sweep out of the cliffs as quick as lightning, and the hand must follow the eye almost by instinct. I have heard men instruct a novice to wait for the boat to rise to a wave, but any such advice I consider unpractical.

I have had splendid pigeon shooting in the north of Ireland, and have found the only method of scoring well is to hold the gun almost up to the shoulder and, the moment a bird is within range, to fire at once, keeping the gun on the move all the time.

It is really best to have only one gun in a boat. I emphasize this as I have seen some dangerous sea shooting by excited youths in boats. No sport is more enjoyable but it demands constant watchfulness and care as long as a cartridge is in the gun. I do not recommend readers to join a pigeon-shooting party in County Donegal, unless they know exactly who is going to shoot with them.

Shooting at sea from a crab-boat in east-coast harbours is really a glorified form of shore shooting, but on the right morning in October or November I am almost sure that even the most fastidious game Shot would not regret a day on the salt water. Indeed, I have repeatedly found that the novelty of the proceeding has frequently lingered long and pleasantly in the memory of a visitor who has come to Norfolk to shoot pheasants and has taken a by-day with me 'up the harbour, across the bar, and out to sea'. On the way, many shots will be obtained at redshank, knot, and other waders, while in sharp weather hard fowl of various species are sure to be encountered.

An open boat on the open sea is not particularly luxurious, but we thought much of the humble bags when I indulged in this sport as a youngster. Carefully would we stroke the feathers of our prizes as we laid them out in rows on the table of the old George when we got home, and proudly would the merganser drake which had so long eluded us, and had at last fallen a victim to youthful prowess, be displayed and then packed up and dispatched to the bird stuffer.

CHAPTER XXII

A Flight to Remember

ALAN SAVORY

COASTAL WILDFOWLING in terms of heavy bags can be one of the most unrewarding occupations. But no true wildfowler ever counts the weight of the bag as the success of the day, because he knows that every now and then there will come a time when all his efforts for, perhaps, an entire season, will be rewarded by a brief period of magic.

It happened this year to me, after many cold hours waiting in the gloomy shelter of ditches and reed-built hides, only to either miss the only shot of the evening or see nothing at all save the darting redwings going to roost in the sallow bushes and hear a brief whisper of ducks' wings far up in the drizzling air. However, on this particular night all the disappointments of the season were made up for. There had been floods out on the marshes all the year and the mallard had sat out on them in thousands, and only came to flight ponds at midnight or not at all. Morning flight on waters that had, from times immemorial, been daylight resting places for hundreds of wildfowl had provided little sport. It is our custom to shoot such places only a very few times each season, and then only from dawn to 8.30 in the morning, so as to cause as little disturbance as possible, and the late arrivals find nothing to frighten them away. This year they were all late, and a great proportion of the fowl just sat out all day on the flooded marsh.

And then, after a long period of calm, wet weather, the wind suddenly went round to the east and began to blow a gale. The flooded waters began to freeze and every inland pool became covered with a hard coating of ice. That night found me within a few hundred yards of a long line of sandhills, fiery in the reddening glow of the setting sun. Beyond was the roaring sea, caged by the marram hills from overflowing the land that reached away as flat as a pancake to a jostling horizon of scrubby bushes and a vast cloud-filled sky that broke and reformed, and let through spears of crimson from the sinking sun.

I was crouched in a hide beside a small pool that was rapidly freezing over and had only two small openings left in the ice. The wind was keen as a knife and there were intermittent snow showers. There were migrant Montagu's harriers riding the wind like gliders in the late afternoon over the marram hills, and a continual passage of redwings seeking shelter in the distant sallow bushes that were tossing like witches' broomsticks in the gale. The roaring of the sea and the wind was like a great organ building up to a crashing *fortissimo*, and the dog and I cowered down in our hide, watching the inland sky shatter and reform and go tearing on in the teeth of the masterful wind.

The first mallard came diving out of the sunset like a sudden black dot, followed by a dozen more which rocked and swirled from side to side of the pool, and then whirled away towards the sea. At the flash of the gun they turned in a split second and were fifty yards away; but more came and more and more. They came straight in, dodging and weaving. It was so cold that the gun almost stuck to my fingers.

Twice duck came right in and sat on the ice by my hide, only to flash away into the darkening sky like rockets when I fired at a couple coming down the gale like skiers on a snow slide. Twice two fell for one shot and went straight through the ice, but for the most part the mallard I shot fell out on the snow thirty yards from the pond. In times like these you must forget the average of kills to cartridges and do the best you can, but there was a pair of duck early on in the flight that suddenly appeared a few yards overhead which I missed as cleanly as if the cartridges had been filled with confetti, and a duck far up in the sky which turned suddenly, and belted off downwind, and fell at the shot like a stone, far off by a sallow bush. Why is it that one makes these fantastic hits and misses in times of storm? It happens to us all, I believe.

The duck were still going over by the time it was too dark to see. I climbed stiffly out of the hide and the dog went completely out of control with excitement. I started to pick up on my own with a torch which suddenly decided to misbehave. It was deep darkness and I had only a thin flickering beam of light, but the dog was back with a duck before I got started. He kept bringing in duck and had ten before I had picked up five. By the time we had finished on the land we had a sackful. Then we had to get the ones out of the pond and broke the ice to get to them. We got four out of the ice, but had to leave the two that had broken through. After a valiant swim the dog came out completely sheeted in ice with a duck in his mouth as stiff as an ice block.

There were still some cartridges left in the bag, and there was the gun and the sack full of duck which by now was frozen to the snow. I could not even lift it onto my back, so I dragged it a hundred yards to the track by the sandhills and waited for my friend with his Land-Rover. Meanwhile, the wind roared and the sea howled like a fiend behind the ramparts. Every now and then the whistling wings of the wildfowl came eerily on the rushing storm. The dog rolled in the snow to get the ice out of his coat, and the gun barrels were too sticky to touch as the frost began to bite deeper and deeper. I waited there in the dark, almost intoxicated with the drama of it all, while the wind roared in the hills and the air was full of snowflakes and stinging sand.

CHAPTER XXIII

Duck in the Sunset
TOWER-BIRD

THE TORN and kaleidoscopic sunsets of late autumn and winter, especially as seen over estuaries and seascapes, often defy description. We associate them with wavering lines and wedges of geese and duck, with fast-travelling flocks of wigeon and ragged mobs of curlew, with knifing winds and biting frosts. They belong to true fowling weather, when the fair-weather gunners are conspicuous by their absence and the great majority of bird watchers have had it until the spring.

But just now, and during the past few weeks, the sunsets we have enjoyed have been almost warming, physically and mentally, though now a feeling of frost in the air creeps on the fowler as he waits for the evening flight. There remain fresh in my mind certain sunsets enjoyed during the past September, and the early days of the present month.

I think the first one really to impress me was when three of us (two being old Essex boys) sat facing a southern estuary with a sunset

98

beginning to stain the western sky to our right. We had been sitting in our positions among the spartina grass for some three hours without having fired a shot between us – not even a curlew or a pigeon had come our way, though we happened to be on the usual flight line of both. The sun sank lower and the evening was as mild and warm as any spring day. Following the afterglow which suffused the estuary in brightness, the last of the gulls from inland passed overhead, some of them jinking as they spied one of us below. The mournful weeping of plover and the occasional distant call of redshank, the bubbling of a feeding curlew and the sharp, harsh voice of a mud-wading heron came from the open muds through which a trickle of making tide was now starting to flow. But not a duck, not even a snipe, showed itself.

The brilliance of the multicoloured sky to the west seemed to have become permanent, until deep dusk finally drew a curtain across it. But before that the word 'duck' had passed from watching man to watching man, and we saw flying swiftly from south to north, two to three gunshots or more away, a lonely clear-cut silhouette against the rich reds, orange, yellow, and greens of the backcloth. 'Looks like a wigeon,' said a voice. 'It's a young mallard,' said another. 'The first pintail I've seen this season,' said the third. The two dogs held their own counsel and said nothing, for man's best friend can be a wise beast. We expected the wigeon-mallard-pintail to turn at the end of the estuary and come streaking back, but saw no more of it. Then, a quarter of an hour or so later, a single teal came from and took the same direction as the wigeon-mallard-pintail, and, like it, did not return.

As the three of us rocked and rolled back towards the village along the narrow, slippery, well holed mud-path among the rushes, none spoke, but I know full well that, though we should have liked to have had a shot or two and a bird each for the larder, none had a complaint. Each had thoroughly enjoyed the long wait, the anticipation, the appreciation of all that an estuary in good weather means to the fowler, and I know too that the sight of those two duck in bold silhouette against the glowing embers of the September sunset had made the day.

It was on the next-but-one evening that I found myself flighting alone as far inland as the tide runs. And for this particular spot I have seldom known the duck at this time of year to flight (for twenty minutes or so) better. I sat among the tall, tasselled reeds facing a splash of floodwater some hundred yards broad. In this the full glory of a flaming sunset was reflected so that it seemed that the whole world in front of me was on fire. As the colours softened and started to fade, the duck began to flight, a few at a time. Snipe rasped overhead, and a green sandpiper called its soft, abrupt notes above me in the greyness. First came two mallard flying round twice before setting their wings and coming straight down on the water at the very edge of the flood, but on the far side of it. Then came five; then two more; then three – all landing tantalizingly well out of shot. For once I had not bothered to bring my decoys, which I generally use at this spot and usually to good effect.

I was hesitating whether to clap my hands and hope that the rising duck would make towards me when I saw two more mallard flying across the sunset and turning towards me (never have I seen so many *pairs* as I have this season, and most I have shot have been young birds, but not always a duck and drake). These birds came right over at full range, and I do not think they intended to land, and may not have seen the duck on the water at the edge of the pool. Over they came and I fired a single shot, bringing down one. Ten minutes later almost the identical thing happened.

Later, I held an inquest with myself as to why I did not manage to get in four shots and maybe bag two couple of duck. I came to the conclusion that watching the duck fly round and then suddenly turn straight over me at almost extreme height, and from a sitting position, concentrating on getting onto one bird and seeing it hit and falling, was cause enough for my being too slow to get onto a second bird. Shooting at a high duck directly overhead is far harder than standing and shooting at one not directly overhead, and a second of time makes all the difference under the circumstances, particularly in a strange light, which must affect sight and judgement as the bird passes from the colours of a fading sunset into the grey-green mistiness of the sky-ceiling overhead. Or am I getting slow with advancing age? I do not think so, as only yesterday I put two barrels into a crow which sounded like one shot.

On the evening sandwiched between those about which I have written there was no colourful sunset. I had gone down to some marshes quite early in the afternoon, well content to spend four or five hours watching and waiting to see if anything was on the move.

It was approaching dusk when I saw two mallard flying round, and, as I was watching them, a wisp of between twenty-five and thirty snipe whizzed overhead and departed. As I kept my eye on the duck, the snipe returned, but I gave them no more than a glance. Yet I noted their progress over very damp ground, and presently they came racing back, but turned when wide of me. It was then that I saw their long necks, and it was then that my brain flashed the word 'teal'. I did not shoot into the brown but had time to choose two birds and get off two quick barrels, when three teal fell like leaves, and a fourth more like a stone, though it was only winged.

It fell into floodwater and the dog jumped the intervening dyke and quickly grabbed the diving bird in shallow water. And there, for some reason I cannot fathom, he stood with his capture in his mouth. The small comet of teal was coming in again and mallard, disturbed by the shot, were circling, some with set wings and dropping down towards the pool. And there stood the flaming Don, regardless of my alternately crooning and cursing voice, and he remained thus motionless, except for wildly wagging tail, until the last of the duck tribe had taken themselves off. I rather fancy that his behaviour was the result of a very bad stinging by nettles; he knew that when he returned with his retrieve, he would have to push his way through the deep fringe of nettles on either bank he had dashed through a few minutes before when it rained teal.

He does not fear nettles in the usual course of events, and will face anything to get at his game. But recently he has hunted out a jungle-like wood for pheasants which is a solid mass of nettles, and one or twice has been so badly stung that he has been almost unconscious of what he is doing, even to the extent of walking away from me with his bird, not knowing what he was about.

CHAPTER XXIV

Beyond the Marsh-heads

ALAN SAVORY

THE VAST areas of sand and mud below the high tide mark are dangerous places for those who do not know their geography, and have but scanty knowledge of the tides or the weather. And it is foolhardy to venture out without a guide far from the marsh-heads. On the east coast of England there are no mountains or hills to give any indication of direction, and after the sun has set, and one is far out on the muds, all the horizon looks alike. One might be in the middle of a vast bowl, the edges of which are slowly growing dim; one half is the sea and one half is the land.

By daylight it seems impossible that one can get lost, but when the light has gone, or if a fog comes down, there is a very great danger of losing one's sense of direction and walking out to sea instead of in the opposite direction, or of wandering off at an angle and getting muddled up with the creeks that run like miniature torrents at low tide, and are thirty-foot death traps as the sea rushes in. There are some nasty big creeks on the North Norfolk coast which meander through the mud and sand that stretches for mile after misty mile at low tide between Blakeney and Wells. They have names such as Stiffkey Freshes, Cabbage Creek, High Sand Creek, and Stone Mell Creek, and they are wide rushing rivers at half-tide.

Where they peter out at low tide, and spread over the sand into the low-tide sea, it is like being in another world. The shore is a thin, dark line, and it is a long, long way off. The sea is a menacing white-laced foaming horror that thunders up the manless miles of beaches like an impotent monster waiting for the change of the tide.

There was a bitter January day long ago, in the time of my old dog Drake, which made me lose much sweat, although it was blowing a wind-frost from the east. It had been easterly weather, as they say in Norfolk, for several days, and there were a lot of wigeon in, but they were hard to get. Drake and I had got across the Morston Freshes and Stiffkey Freshes, and then saw a bunch of wigeon in the harbour at the end of Blakeney Point. I left the dog sitting on my bag some way back on the sand, which was blowing like a drifting, white, knee-high curtain, and tried to stalk them. There were a few brent geese with them, and they were very uneasy. I crawled along towards the side of the harbour, which was well above the water at this state of the tide, but when I was about fifty yards away they all flew up. I had a sort of forlorn shot and one wigeon dropped back into the water. Drake rushed up and dashed into the harbour after the bird, which had dived while I stood ready to shoot it again as soon as it surfaced. We waited a long time, but did not see it, and I went back for my bag.

Then we followed the harbour out to the sea, in case the wigeon had gone down with the tide. It was a considerable way to the harbour mouth, and we saw it again just before we got there. Drake went in after it right on the harbour bar, all amongst the breakers. He was in the sea almost a quarter of an hour. I stood in the surf as deep as I dare go, with the backwash pulling against my legs, almost demented. I never thought he would get back, as he went out beyond the first line of breakers, still ploughing after the bird.

When he was in the trough of the waves I could not see him. Then I saw the wigeon dive again right on the crest of a wave, and Drake appeared on the next crest with it in his mouth. He came ashore with the wave in a white smother of thundering foam, and I almost got sucked back into the sea as I grabbed at him to help him up the beach. I was scared stiff over the whole business, and we sat on the

103

blowing sand at the edge of the sea and ate lunch. I felt as limp as a rag, and Drake had all my sandwiches; there was only a banana left in the bag and he did not seem to want that, so I ate it myself.

The sky was a leaden grey, and the far pine trees of Wells seemed to float above the seething surface of the sand and the blowing spray. There were masses of wigeon sitting on the sand, and parties of brent flew along beyond the breakers. Once or twice I thought I saw long streamers of scoter duck skimming the waves far out.

After a while the wind seemed to get a bit back into the north, and the sea began to get steeper. A great gobbet of froth came right up to us and I realized that the tide had turned and was pouring in like a great yeasty torrent. One could not keep pace with it by walking fast; it just poured in as if someone had turned on a giant tap. I started to run alongside the harbour. The sand seemed to be getting wet and sticky and the sea roared exaltingly behind us. The saltings appeared to be miles away. I can remember saying to myself, 'Keep running you fool; keep running.' We just about made the Stiffkey Freshes, but the Morston Freshes were too deep by the mussel-beds and we had to follow them up beyond the sluice doors to where it has, or had, a rickety wooden bridge and a stony bottom between the Stiffkey meal marshes and the greens by the boundary fence.

The frost was only a wind-frost and did not last, but it brought the mallard out of the inland lakes and that night I shot one from the knoll on the Morston Marshes where we had gone to lie down in the high grass to get out of the wind for a while.

There is a place far out on the sands somewhere between High Sand Creek and Stone Mell Creek that is called Blacknock. It is a patch of mud covered with eel-grass, and full of blue-shelled cockles known as 'Stewkey blues'. It is a famous place for wigeon, but very dangerous to get on to and off, if one is not too certain of the way on a dark night. The women cockle gatherers from Stiffkey (or Stewkey, as it is sometimes called), who have double the strength of a normal man, go right out there between the tides and get a peck of these cockles and carry them back to the village, miles across the sand and saltings. Some time during the early 1900s, one of these almost superhuman women got caught by the tide on Blacknock. A fog came on suddenly and she could not find her way back. The whelk boats from Wells got caught in it out at sea and came in all along the coast. The crews said they could hear the woman screaming in the fog on Blacknock. She took hours to drown in the shallow seething water, and the terrible screaming went on and on all night, and they could not find her in the fog.

Next day she was there, drowned on Blacknock. They say that on foggy nights, when the sea moves uneasily beneath its white blanket, and the gulls forsake the outer sand-bars, you can hear her screaming still. A friend of mine said that if you sit on Blacknock by moonlight, when there is a thin mist and all is quiet, the myriads of cockles, opening below their spit-holes in the mud, makes such a sighing and a sobbing that you can imagine anything.

There used to be a piece of an old wreck by Cabbage Creek. The sea had carved out a deep, blue-black hole all round it. One day a friend and myself took a butt-fork out there. A butt-fork is a trident on the end of a long pole used for catching flatfish in the creeks. We could just about reach the bottom of this ghastly-looking pool with the fork, and we pricked into something that almost kicked the shaft out of our hands. We quite thought it was a giant conger and prepared for a battle royal, but, when we at last managed to haul in the butt-fork, we found that we had spiked a 3 ½-lb flat-fish. It was a beauty, and we had it for tea that night at The Morston Anchor.

There was another wreck at the mouth of Blakeney harbour. She was a collier, and she went ashore one roaring dark night during the First World War. All the crew were drowned except one man, who fought his way through the smother of icy surf and landed on Blakeney Point, and, smothered in blood, blundered into the watch-house where the lookout crew were playing cards and almost killed them with fright. At low water one could board this wreck and lie on the deck and look through the dim green ghostly depths of the hold, and watch the gillie-crabs climbing up the limpet-encrusted sides.

Anything could have lived down there, from a devil fish to a giant conger, but one summer day when the terns were diving after the whitebait in the low-tide summer sea, the saltings were a purple haze of sea lavender, and the pine trees of Wells were shimmering in the mirage above the Stiffkey high sands, I was fishing from one of Bill Temple's boats by the harbourmouth when three children appeared over the sand, two boys of about fourteen and a girl of perhaps ten. They had a great game of pirates on this old wreck, and took turns to dive into the hold after treasure. I would not have done it if there had been any treasure – not for a fortune in gold blocks or Spanish doubloons!

CHAPTER XXV

Mistake by Moonlight

MICHAEL SHEPHARD

THE MEANS of humiliation for a shooting man are almost limitless
– the low pigeon missed which becomes tall and is taken cleanly
by your companion; the fast-moving rabbit bowled over neatly by your
neighbour as it reaches the hedge after your two wandering barrels
have inspired its speed; the wild duck that pitched in front of you
and waited, yet. . . . Yes, most of us have known such moments.

But quite the most brutal experience anyone could have, anyone,
that is, who shares my affliction of goose fever, befell me last January
about an hour after the moon had risen.

We had gathered in a comfortable hostelry close by our marsh and
had laid our plans for six days of goose hunting. We were six – the
senior member, the expert, the young entry, the schoolmaster, the
novelist and myself.

On arrival, we were informed by the watcher that there were
few geese about and that they were getting fewer, one of those

unaccountable local migrations being in progress. However, he had been feeding the birds on one marsh and reported that about two hundred had been visiting it regularly for two weeks – so regularly, indeed, that once the moon period had started the geese had come in while he and his young son were still distributing the rotten potatoes over the marsh. 'They just circled round us until we left and were feeding before we got out of sight,' he told us.

Next morning we breakfasted at leisure and pottered about the marshes during the day, looking for feathers and droppings. The feeding ground presented the most unusual appearance, fouled by droppings and bedraggled feathers to an extent I have never experi-enced before. The area covered by the potatoes was comparatively small and the watcher had replenished the supply in the same places each time.

My immediate reaction was that he would have been better advised to move his feeding gradually, so that the birds could return to reasonably fresh ground each day, for I am sure that geese do not like feeding on stale ground. However, as the watcher pointed out, he had managed to hold some geese on that marsh, although they had left the rest of the area. Furthermore, it was the one place that provided a little natural cover in all that waste of desolate grassland and rhines.

The day had been clear and as the moon was only three days from the full we quite expected the first geese to arrive before dusk as they had done under similar conditions the year before. However, the marshman had told us that the whole lot (he said five hundred) had left together soon after eleven o'clock that morning – just before we had reached the marsh. During the day we had seen no geese at all, so it did seem that the whole lot would probably come back together at about six o'clock, as they had been doing for the past few days.

We settled down to wait soon after four o'clock – the schoolmaster, the expert, the young entry and I. The novelist had gone off on his own, and the senior member had found another likely spot where the evidence of fresh droppings suggested that something might well come his way.

The cover I referred to was two hummocks, rather like barrows, with a rabbit warren on top. By day they were bald, but they produced some sort of shadow at night until the moon was high in the sky. The expert and the schoolmaster occupied these strategic points, while the young entry sought the shelter of a broken gate where a track crossed the rhine, and I lay uncomfortably against the steep, damp bank of the rhine about a hundred yards below him. Between the rhine and the hummocks were about a hundred yards of open marsh where the potatoes had been scattered.

Knowing a little about the habits of the geese that visit our marshes, we agreed that they would probably follow the line of the river inland and, as a fair breeze was blowing from the river to us, turn into the marshes some distance above or below the feeding place, taking a big arc to bring them into the wind for their approach and landing. From our positions the Guns in the shelter of the hummocks or I myself should be able to get a shot, and the young entry would be almost certain of the chance of killing his first goose as the alarmed birds climbed away.

Well, now, intelligent anticipation, thinking like a goose and laying careful ambushes for the birds are of great assistance to the goose hunter when successful. But it is as well to allow for a multitude of varying contingencies, any one of which may bring about a change in the behaviour of the geese.

We had been waiting about an hour when the duck began to come in and for once, because we had agreed to save our powder and the peace of the marsh for geese alone, there were a great many duck flying down the rhine, low and clearly seen against the pale veil of wispy cloud that had gathered.

First of all teal began to call round the marsh, their shrill piping coming closer until a dimly seen shape hurled low across the rhine to pitch on a small patch of dabble in the centre of the feeding ground. Then the mallard came over in small parties, flying steadfastly into the wind and straight over my head. Finally we heard the wigeon all the way from the estuary and for a full half-hour parties of them wandered backwards and forwards, round and round above the marsh, many of them over our heads.

The 6.10 train travelled its way along the edge of the estuary, hurling a myriad sparks to the sky, and I was watching it vaguely when the call of a goose from way down river made me forget the discomfort of my ditch and pressed me tight against the slight bank of mud.

I did not see them, but later the young entry told me that there were only two and that they flew straight up the river. I heard their voices dwindling, and no more. They did not swing back and our expectancy dwindled, too. The discomfort made itself felt again.

My watch showed me that it was well past 7.30 when a low whistle drew my attention to the shadows that gathered by the dabble on the marsh. There had been a warning, for a minute or so before several duck had clattered off, protesting to the night.

I joined my friends for a short council of war and accepted the proffered flask, but it was no sooner against my lips than a single goose called from the river. We stood still and then, as the full babble of a big skein broke out, we ran to new positions.

There was no question of reaching our shelter, for the birds were on top of us; we ran with the common thought that dispersal might produce the chance of a shot for someone and that our group was far too conspicuous, even at night.

Fumbling to screw back the cap of the flask, which I had absent-mindedly retained, I felt naked and exposed as the moon was uncovered by the drifting clouds. On a previous occasion, both whitefronts and pinkfeet had come to our guns confidently under similar circumstances, but this time they saw us. There can be no other explanation for their conduct. There were two big parties and they were very low as they circled out of gunshot.

At first it did look as if they would come into the wind and over us, but the chatter ceased abruptly and the birds started another circuit. They were obviously excited, and continued to circle for over twenty minutes, sometimes diving, almost tumbling to the marsh with an explosive rush of air through their pinions, then climbing and turning away.

At first we stood still and then, when it was too late, made for cover. Had we done that the moment we had heard them, all would have been over but the shooting.

Tiring of their little game and prompted by hunger, both parties headed back to the river and followed its course upstream, chattering loudly. They did not go far, however, before their voices betrayed their movement into the marsh, and after a short while they seemed to have gone down.

Once again we came together and, thinking I knew where the birds were feeding, I suggested that I should get round them and put them up while the others waited under cover.

I stalked round the field I had in mind, and searched it with my binoculars without seeing the sign of a goose. I was about to leave the rhine and advance across the marsh again when I heard the geese calling. They were circling the marsh beyond me and I decided to call them myself.

You cannot teach anyone to call a goose by the written word, and I do not think that I am very good at it but my call was answered and

I played canny, not calling again until the question in the voice of the one goose that had answered me seemed imperative. Again I gave that sharp but subdued note and soon afterwards knew that the geese *had* turned and *were* coming to me.

They came noisily and I peered into the gloom above the moonlit marshland. They came low, so low that I did not see them until they were in range and almost over me. Of course, control and common sense went to the wind and I fired blindly at the great shadows that crossed me closer than any goose will ever fly to me again.

How I reviled myself as they went away! Not only had I spoiled my own chance, but I had deprived the others of the chances I had set out to get for them. But, no – two shots echoed across to me and three more.

Not a minute later I heard the second party coming down river and once again I called them in. Again they came low, but not directly over me; they were about thirty feet up, and about forty feet from me when they crossed the rhine in line abreast – some forty great shapes just asking to be enfiladed. But my humiliation had been too great, and I allowed them to pass on towards the others without raising my gun.

However, before they had gone half the distance to the waiting Guns they turned back to the river and no shot disturbed their progress. My humiliation was now complete, but when I saw the dark silhouettes of my friends gathered together on top of the hummocks it turned to irritation, only slightly dispelled when I found that they had gathered to admire the four pinkfeet which they had just retrieved. The expert said, 'After you fired, they climbed steadily and came over perfectly,' and the young entry, picking up his first goose, said 'Thank you, Michael' – so I kept my feelings to myself.

CHAPTER XXVI

─◆─

Sometimes Perfect

MICHAEL SHEPHARD

'I DON'T THINK there's a hope of getting one with the weather like this,' I said, 'but we'll hear them and we'll see them. You know what it is?' And the others, their minds flashing back to barren dawns on the Solway, the Humber, and the Wash, were readily able to picture an empty morning on the Severn. 'But, of course, it's sometimes perfect,' I added.

They had come a long way to shoot with me, had Berry and Mac, and, as so often happens, the weather had changed for the worst – it was fair instead of foul. But the alarm clock marked the turn of the tide of expectancy at 4 a.m. and life could not have been more pleasant as we ate our breakfast in the old stone kitchen. It would be enough to hear the geese for the first time of the season, to see their twisting lines etched faintly against the dawn in the distance. My latest news was that there were about a thousand on the river, so I felt sure that we would see them, but 'hope springs eternal', as the poet said, and I think that each one of us was hoping for that single skein which follows its own course instead of proceeding according to the communal plan.

It was still night when we reached the swing bridge over the canal. It was dark enough to make navigation difficult as we crossed the marsh, and one deep rhine lay dangerously before us with no sign of the little bridge that I remembered. Berry flashed his torch and said, 'It's quite shallow; we can wade it,' and plunged down the bank. So we waited for a few minutes while he extricated first one leg and then the other from the deep and embracing mud which lies beneath a trickle of water – a trap for the unwary. We worked our way round and reached the bank above the river with the shrilling of redshank and the call of curlew coming as a thrill and an almost new sensation. We sensed the air, wished each other 'straight powder' and separated to our hiding places under the overhanging bank of a drain.

For half an hour there was no other sound but the calling waders and the harsh, mocking chatter of shelduck far out on the sands where, perhaps, the geese were stirring. Above the hills in the east a glorious green light began to spread; over the faint blur of the western uplands towards Wales the south-west wind started to bank cloud masses as it seems to do at almost every dawn on the Severn. But there was no thrilling whisper of wings as duck returned from the fresh marshes, no mutter of goose talk from the muds and sand-bars.

I wondered what would happen, whether they would come at all to bathe our senses in the delight of the sight and sound of them. I wondered whether some small party might offer a chance to Mac's magnum, or Berry's double-8, but I had little real hope that my own game gun would be required. As the light grew behind us I felt some anxiety, for still there was no sound of geese; even the waders were silent and the shelduck had stifled their laughter. The dawn was pregnant with silence as the first drops of rain began to fall and the clouds veiled the rising but dying moon.

Then, suddenly, all was well as a brief chattering cackle came from low over the marsh to my right – uncertain and impossible to place. Then it came again from behind me and faded towards the canal as I realized that Berry had crept up to me to ask whether I had seen them – thirteen flying low, but well out from our hiding places. Somehow I felt that geese were coming rather than heard them, and I urged my friend to get back to his own place. I wish I had kept him with me.

Flying slowly, steadily, but very silently for whitefronts, the geese passed over my head. A perfect V of nine at seventy yards, a ragged party of five at sixty, another big lot only thirty yards above the marsh, but fifty yards to my right, and then a skein right over my head, but just too tall for my ounce of No. 5. If only the big guns, my guests, had been there – but they were not and Berry watched the birds passing at an angle which put them too far out to his right, although he was only forty yards from me. And Mac? He did not even know there were any geese on our side, but watched other skeins just skipping over the sea-wall two hundred yards down river. Then they were passed, but the clamour of their calling as they weaved about the feeding grounds, whiffled excitedly above the elms, set their wings to land, only to raise them again to make another circuit, and the babble of their voices remained. We had seen them and could still see the intricate tracery of the circling skeins against the yellowing green of that strange dawn. We had heard them and could still hear them as that wild chorus rose in crescendo, dwindled and rose again.

Two geese broke away from that great anserine air display. Two geese drifted across the marsh towards me and turned close by the wire fence beyond the drain. One dropped its head and wings at my shot, flapped wildly, and disappeared against the shadow which persisted close to the marsh. I forgot my second barrel as the other goose rose into the wind and turned away.

Well, there it was. Mac and I concentrated on Berry, who had the tea in his gamebag. Then I set off as the light grew strong to find my 'wounded' goose, but returned disconsolate after half an hour's wandering and searching with the binoculars. All the time geese were moving over the distant trees. It is extraordinary how long they will take to settle down to their feeding, even in a sanctuary, especially if the food has no particularly strong appeal. I might have saved myself the walk and the temporary disappointment, for both my companions were sure that the bird was dead, and they had been able to see it for longer than me. Mac and I walked across to the point where he had seen it drop and, sure enough, there it was on the grass, wings outstretched and head forward, dead within forty yards of the empty cartridge which I had ejected on the bank of the rhine. It was a grand old whitefront with heavy breast barring and a big patch of white extending from the base of the bill for an inch and half on to the crown.

For a while we sat on the bank, talking and watching the geese down the marsh, the shelduck out on the muds and a line of teal on the edge of a little gutter. The approach of a cormorant caused one sudden alarm and sent us to action stations, for Berry had put out my goose as a decoy in case its mate came back looking for it, as so often they do. Whitefronts are not easily decoyed, but occasionally a lone bird can be brought in. A jet aircraft passed low over the farmlands beyond the canal and some seven hundred geese rose in panic, toured the marsh, and returned to their feeding – a magnificent sight as they swung down against the rosy sunrise, the sort of picture you do not quite believe when it appears on canvas.

The chance of another shot was remote. I had only seen one party of geese go up river so it was unlikely that more than that would come back and, if those did, they would almost certainly be out of range. Later in the season, when the geese are wandering more in search of grazing, it is possible to get a shot at all odd hours as they drift back to the sands or the sanctuary. But this day only twenty-odd had gone up river and the chance of them coming back over us within the hour that remained was slight, of their coming within range even slighter.

Yet these things do happen. Sitting there on the grass, feet dangling over the steep bank, watching a large concourse of curlew twisting in to the fresh marsh and flocks of lapwing flying high, following the flight of a party of rooks as they headed along the canal, we saw the thin wispy line appear above the trees near the old church two miles away. They were geese, geese coming back and, at that distance, geese coming straight to us. But, of course, they were too high.

We did not move – just watched them growing against the clear sky from which the clouds had been carried by the wind. But that wind was not strong enough to force the birds down. Yet they did seem to be losing height, or was it wishful thinking? Like a trio of race commentators we kept our glasses up and shared the running commentary, each hoping against hope that this was a day of miracles. Then it really did seem that there might be a chance, and, without a word, we moved together, slipping back behind the bank, hiding binoculars and thermoses and cups under the gamebag and checking our guns.

I still wonder at it. The skein was dropping but it would pass to the right. It altered course as one goose talked. It came straight to us, the birds about sixty-five yards high and beyond the range of my puny weapon. But I saw Mac raise his magnum as the geese were overhead; Berry still crouched, and did not move his gun until the magnum fired. There was a great outcry of protest and the skein wheeled towards the river as it climbed, but one dropped lower and fell beyond our sight, out on the muds.

Berry was on his feet with a shout of 'Instantly dead in the air, sir' – a private joke of ours – and then I knew that our day had been made as I ran with Mac to get his goose.

Berry's bird had fallen on hard sand, but Mac's was out on the soft, shifting and treacherous ooze beyond the channel, which now, at low tide, was easily forded. Mac had only moved about twenty paces when he stuck; I found a slightly better path and did eventually reach the goose. Berry stood on the bank with his in his hand and gave valuable advice which was lost on the wind. Then the fight back, with thoughts of those who were unlucky in the past and found quicksands. By the time I reached the wall I could only put down the goose and stand doubled up in the channel, sickened by the exertion. Mac, too, had only then extricated himself and his long boots from the estuary's embrace.

Away over the farms the jet flew low and scattered the feeding birds so that once and again it seemed that we should have more shots before we turned for home. But as they approached us, only to turn away beyond range, our concealment was half-hearted and one or the other voiced the feelings of the three of us: 'I don't particularly want to shoot any more.' If they *had* come in range, well, that would have been a different matter; but it could not have improved the pleasure and thrill of that morning. A goose apiece, a shot apiece for big gun, magnum, and the little one. Goose shooting is sometimes perfect!

CHAPTER XXVII

Joe's Goose

JOHN HUMPHREYS

IT WAS in about 1960 that I became aware of his existence. I met him plodding off the Solway marshes on a cold January morning at a lonely stretch on the Scottish side called Cummertrees. Like me, he was a winter visitor, a once-a-year goose man who had made the pilgrimage to the fowler's Mecca, lured by the clamour of the great skeins, the lowering bulk of Griffel, the smell of salt mud and the primitive urge of the hunter.

His name was Joe and he worked in a bank, his clerkly spectacles and balding head seeming to suit his profession perfectly. Joe had read of the magic of fowling and, in the family Morris Minor, made his long, lonely journey far from his native Hertfordshire, stayed in the local guest-house and spent his mornings, evenings and sometimes his days too waiting patiently on the shore for just a chance at one of the great grey birds.

He was not a rich man as the world measures such things, but his fowling gear had been bought carefully, with money no object. He

116

wore a Barbour Solway smock, that old champion of wildfowling coats (now, sadly, no longer available), long boots, scarf and gloves, and was festooned with all the usual accoutrements. Binoculars hung from his neck and he sported a sound Birmingham magnum and used Eley magnum cartridges loaded with BB, a popular goose load in those days.

Joe always chose the first week of the new year for his fowling holiday, as indeed did I, and for many years after that I was to meet him on his way to or from his favourite creek and we would exchange a few words. In all the time I knew him he shot no goose, for by a cruel quirk of fate they always passed by to either side of him or flew at great range overhead. He essayed the occasional shot but, through a combination of bad marksmanship and bad luck, consistently failed to score and drove back south at the end of his week with nothing tangible to take home, no sop to silence the jests of wife and children on his return.

But he was not deterred, for the magic of goose fever was in his blood and, sure enough, next year he would be there again with hope rekindled in his breast.

Then one year I noticed that Joe had bought a new 10-bore gun, a long-chambered monster which took the full load and which, he explained, would give him the edge he lacked and might produce for him a goose from one of those skeins which always flew too high. But even this improved firepower was not to be the answer, for at the end of his week I found myself once more commiserating with him for his lack of luck. 'Never mind,' he would say, 'better luck next year. I am determined to bag one of those things before they carry me out feet first.'

It was in his fifteenth season that success finally came to Joe.

During those years he had travelled thousands of weary miles, spent money he could ill afford on his equipment, suffered the discomfort of moderate lodgings, withstood the ravages of fifteen Scottish Januaries and faced the taunts of family, friends and colleagues at his lack of a trophy. The lure remained strong enough for him to withstand all that. One day he would have his goose and bring it proudly home, to be photographed with him clutching it by the neck and, when all the celebrating was over, it would be eaten with all due ceremony.

Then came the day, the last of his week in 1975, as I recall, when the snow lay thinly on the Solway grass, the great mountain top blushed pink in the sunrise and a thin wind swept in from the sea half a mile away. The great skeins had gone clamouring in miles high and, just when we thought it was all over, a small party of pinks left the sand and beat a steady course towards where Joe crouched in his gutter. I was a quarter of a mile away, but could see clearly what happened next.

On and on they came until it seemed they had passed him by, but then one goose lurched and planed off and away from the main group and then I heard the double shot of the 10-bore floating down to where I too lay in hiding.

In an instant, Joe was out of his hide. I could imagine his feelings, his fierce elation. The moment he had awaited so long, with such dogged patience, had at long last arrived. The bird glided down far off over a creek, and, what was more, it was a strong runner and Joe had no dog. Fowling was one thing but his wife drew the line at a muddy spaniel on her good carpets.

He set off running like a redshank, his bag flapping on his back. It was a long chase with some nifty dodging and doubling at the end of it, but at last he swooped triumphantly and fell on his bird where it crouched in the lavender. By now he was a distant figure but I could see him plodding back with the precious burden cradled in his arms. My heart warmed for the old boy: success at last, and well deserved.

I wandered over to his hide to offer my congratulations, for by now the flight was truly over. I was surprised at what I saw, but should not have been, for it explained much of the odd illogicality, the crazy and inexplicable relationship between the hunter and hunted which our opponents simply cannot grasp.

Joe had taken off his Solway Smock, baring his shirt to the searing wind. There was a smear of mud on his spectacles and he was still panting from the unaccustomed exercise. Lovingly wrapped up in his coat, its head and neck protruding long and snakelike but its brown eyes quite unafraid, was a large pinkfoot. Joe looked at me, the light of battle and exhilaration gleaming from his bifocals. He spoke through chattering teeth as gently he stroked the grey feathers.

'It's only wingtipped; I think I can save it. Do you know the whereabouts of the nearest vet?'

Fenland sunset *Jonathan Yule*

Wigeon under a full moon *Julian Novorol*

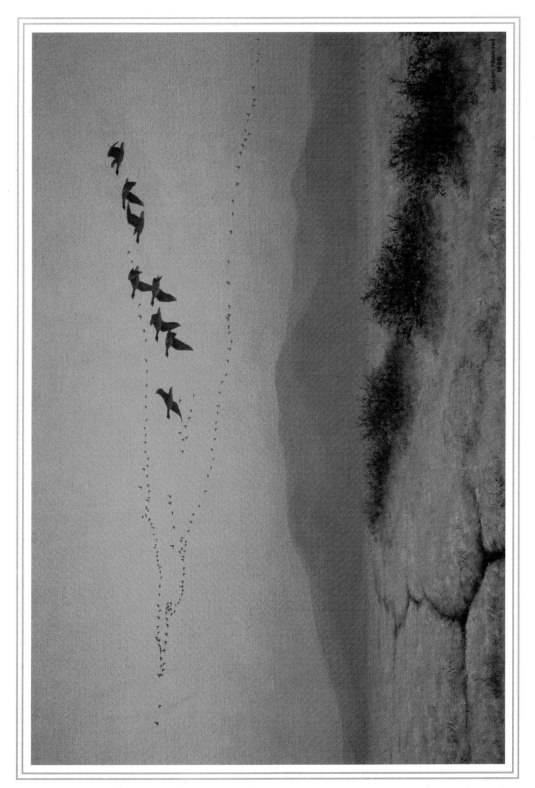

Sunset over the Solway – pinkfeet flighting out over the whins *Julian Novorol*

Down with the tide on the Dee – punt gunning *Julian Novorol*

Pintail at Cley Marshes *Jonathan Yule*

Barnacles against Criffel – Solway *Julian Novorol*

California Snows   Geoffrey Campbell-Black

Brent along the tide *Julian Novorol*

CHAPTER XXVIII

Ten-bore Wigeon

JOHN HUMPHREYS

H IS VAN squelched to a halt alongside the pile of rotting straw bales as snugly as a calf stands beside its mother. The man switched off lights and motor and sat for a moment while his eyes adjusted to the purple bloom of the night and his ears to the subtler sounds than the clattering of his engine, which still clicked and ticked as it cooled. The contrast caused by the sudden cessation of the jolting and bumping of his ride down the pock-marked lane gave him an uncanny feeling of otherworldliness; the noises and the lurching of his journey had at least occupied his mind and held at bay the slight twinge of loneliness which now assailed him.

His pupils dilated enough for him to distinguish between the black bowl of the sky and the blacker mass beneath it which was the sea-wall. His ears tuned more finely to catch the breath of wind which rustled the straw and the distant wail of a peewit. Old Fen fowlers, living as they did in times of superstition and strange fears, must have been

119

either brave men or devoid of any imagination to have even ventured out in the dark.

With a conscious effort he tugged at the door handle and heaved himself out into the night. The tang of salty mud and sea lavender would have told even a blind man that he was near the sea. The man opened the back of his van and his dog, a great raw-boned extrovert of a black labrador, leaped out and pranced about him before dashing off to the nearest inanimate object. With his appearance the remaining wisp of the man's morbid and primitive fears left him. The bustle of donning oilskins, belt, bag, scarf and the hopping about on one leg trying to pull on a reluctant wader were done in increasing haste as a new emotion of eager anticipation crept upon him.

Old habit made him check before leaving to make sure that his vehicle was safe despite the unlikelihood of another wanderer passing this spot on a winter's morn. He had everything: compass, torch and whistle for emergencies; ammunition and, most important, his long-chambered double 10-bore, a gun whose beautiful damascene was hammered out long before he was born but which with loving care and pride he maintained in perfect order.

He followed the familiar path out across the saltings, stepping firmly but with care over the narrow gutters which, with their surprising depth and treacherous overhang, could throw down a man and break his leg. His dog knew better than to gallop about but plodded at heel, head down to sniff at the tide wrack or to investigate hopefully the spartina for signs of any other canine travellers. There was plenty of time for reflection and the man thought of all the other fowlers who had shot this part of the Norfolk coast in the great old days of goose shooting. Why, fifty years ago a man had killed geese from the very High Street of nearby Wells and famous and infamous gunners had lain up in the sand with their eights and fours in the hope of sending a goose crashing down into the pine trees behind them. They had gone now, both geese and gunners – the latter as often as not to graves on distant battlefields and the former first farther round the coast and later to the secluded sea lochs and mosses of Scotland.

The marsh remained constant during these ephemeral changes – as constant, that is, as can any salt marsh of mud and sand which alters slightly with every rip tide that pushes the salt and shingle to and fro. The eastern sky grew less dark, redshank belled, and now he could see gulls, cold and angular, winging over, wheeling and keening when they saw the plodding figure below. The man reached the edge of the green marsh and stood on a little island of spartina surrounded by a maze of wide creeks. Brown mud, rich and soft, stretched away before him like the wind-ribbed sands of a great desert. He cast about for a place to hide and settled for the lip of a great creek where a minor hedge of sea lavender gave him a hint of protection. Into this recess man and dog snuggled as though it were the softest bed on earth.

He checked his great gun to see that the muzzles were clear of mud and to make sure that it was loaded, then he couched it in a bed of grass ready to hand but not conspicuous to sharp eyes above. Almost immediately there was a flicker of wings and a little trip of dunlin came flashing past and settled in the creek outfall, probing and running hither and thither on twinkling legs. The sky grew lighter by the minute, a jagged rent appeared in night's cloak and the apple-green and pink lining tinged the east.

The man pricked his ears – geese, surely! There was no mistaking that subdued murmur punctuated by the shrill shout of an old gander. The sound came and went on the breeze, as tantalizing as The Piper at the Gates of Dawn in *The Wind in the Willows*. The small skein, descendants perhaps of the Wells geese of old, passed unseen and faded shorewards. It had been a sound to set the pulses racing and the man felt a return of the unease he had felt earlier. How could the simple cry of a common bird affect modern, sophisticated man in this way?

It was brent next, croaking and flapping raggedly along the now making tide which he could just see as a white line creeping over the ooze. Curiously, there was not the same emotion for this sound, although the birds were indeed geese and as wild and unapproachable as any greys. Perhaps they lost some of their magic when the mantle of official protection fell upon them so long ago. The bird has certainly proliferated since, and the local gunners complained that they ruined the few remaining eel-grass beds and with them the local wigeon shooting.

The thought was barely in his mind when it was wigeon that he saw, not too high, about a score of them bearing up to him obliquely across the mud. A silver whistle floated downwind as his hand snaked to the pistol grip of the great gun. There was no time to think for the moment was upon him as they crossed in front; another second and it would be too late. The 10-bore spoke once, twice, with belch of flame and acrid black-powder smoke. From the middle of the flight two birds peeled out and smacked into the plum-cake mud. The dog ran in and had them back in a twinkling – two cocks, their white breasts sullied by the mud into which they had plumped with such finality.

It was time to go. The sun was up and soon the tide would fill the creeks behind him and cut off his retreat. He walked back quickly, making light work of the path he had trodden so gingerly before sunrise. He carried his birds by the necks rather than crumple and dirty them further in his capacious bag. He crossed the last creek, now filling rapidly, with but inches to spare at his wader tops. The tower of his parish church gave him a sure landmark; now he was safe. He turned to gaze back at the marsh and gave it a long, lingering look as if drinking in its wild but subdued beauty and its desolation, enough to last him another week in the city bustle where he was obliged to make his living.

That done, he marched off briskly, dog at heel, in search of the van.

CHAPTER XXIX

———◆———

A Pattern of Wings

JONATHAN YOUNG

FIFTY YEARS ago, when the great herring fleets emptied their slippery treasure into Great Yarmouth, the pinkfeet sailed the flat skies above Wells in their thousands. In their trail came a second migration – of goose hunters. Gentlemen gunners, Cambridge undergraduates and the professional fowlers thronged the dunes armed with every kind of ordnance. Four-bores, double 8s, 10s, long-chambered 12s – every conceivable goose gun was employed to knock a space out of a skein and send its occupant spinning earthwards.

For years the geese withstood the pressure. Then they stopped coming, their place taken by strings of brent. Once eagerly pursued, the black goose of the punt-gunners now cronks unperturbed past the seaside trippers drinking their thick tea out of white china in the little teashops. Then, one day, a few years ago, the grey geese decided to return. A small party flighted over the pines at Holkham late one October. The following season they brought their companions. The scouting parties became an army. Today they flight in their thousands, and the skies are filled with great chunks of geese.

Mid-November. Thirty or so blackbirds are guzzling fallen apples. The night frosts have been hard; they'll need every scrap of energy. These short winter afternoons have an awkward hour after lunch and before setting off for the marsh. We scratch about making tea, talking goose loads. The dog picks up the expectant tension and begins mooching round the door.

The blackbirds are *chink-chinking*, signalling the steady erosion of light as we clump our way towards the shore. Cold air mixes with the pine resin and the salt to produce the characteristic smell of the Holkham Gap. On the sands parents gather their children and head homewards, having walked off their lunch. Farther off, a young couple throw sticks for their dog.

We splash our way through a long pool and settle down in the dunes. Unsleeving our guns, we load up. I push in a couple of heavy-load No. 3s, wipe the sand from the action and close the gun. It makes a ghastly grating sound, hardly surprising since it's almost impossible to prevent the sand getting in here. It reminds me of the last time I had the gun serviced; the gunsmith mentioned that it was not usual for a boxlock to contain barnacles and a piece of crab.

It's really cold now. A fresh easterly has the North Sea booming onto the sand and the skin tightening on our faces. Somehow, inevitably, the wind curls down my collar. The dog hurls itself over the dune, growling manically. A poodle's topknot juts round the ridge followed by the couple we saw earlier. Clad in mud-spattered waxproofs and waders, our guns cradled in our laps, we present a strange apparition. But they anticipate our greeting with a cheery 'You're flighting then? Well, we'll go down the other side of the beach. Good luck!' Good place, Norfolk. People actually understand wildfowling.

A single goose flights high over, a feral greylag joining its brethren on Holkham Lake. A dunlin alights feet away, primps and scurries round for a last bite. Eleven brent slide through the wind barely ten feet up. We can practically touch them. Not a sign, though of the pinks. Not a solitary high yelp.

The greyness turns slate then dark-blue. Very rarely is it truly pitch black. A navigation buoy sparks its message. A haze of yellow light appears around Wells. Families, returned from their outings, are sipping hot tea and munching crumpets. It's bitingly cold.

Orion, the Plough, Sirius, the Pole Star – each materializes and takes its ordered place. Every few minutes a meteor arcs its path briefly. They're all out now, the whole shining mass, the Milky Way worn like a sash through its middle. No sign yet, though, of the moon, or of any cloud. Without both a single goose can fly within feet and yet still be invisible. The beach is deserted, no movement save the surf and the wind. The geese aren't going to flight. We ease our stiffened legs, gather up the hound and head back.

Then I hear them, distantly baying over Holkham Marshes. Waders flapping, we scuttle back to the dunes. A great ragged wave of pinkfeet, hundreds of feet up, sing their wild song and merge into the blackness.

124

Another band of geese pass over, then another. They are far too high for the shot. The last of their cries are crushed by the surf. They leave an air of desolation. Before they flighted we had our expectation to keep us company. After their departure we are left only with the beach, the wind and the stars.

Again we begin to trudge home. Wait! A lighter note chimes through the stillness. Whitefronts! Again we settle into our dunes and hiss at the hound to hup. Five hundred yards out, we guess, and they are heading straight for us. We click off our safeties. The cry of the geese is now all-embracing. They must be so close. But where? We hear the swish of their pinions but see only the stars. With guns half-mounted, we stare until our eyes ache, then catch a glimpse of the end of the skein etched against the Milky Way. They are gone before we can shoot.

A singleton, calling wildly, clambers after the skein. He is no more than yards away but remains unseen. It is impossible to shoot and so we sleeve our guns, lie back in the dunes and watch as the skeins drift over the skies, a pattern of wings touching the pattern of stars.

We have kept our appointment, the hunters and the quarry. Tonight is theirs and we are happy with that.

CHAPTER XXX

Ice-strewn Waters

JONATHAN YOUNG

SLOWLY, TETHERED at her bow and stern, she slithered down the last two feet of bank and sat on the water sulking at her ignominious launching. A redshank, alarmed, shrieked hysterically up river, breaking the grey stillness. It had nothing to fear. The double-handed punt was intended for nobler quarry. Sweating, slipping, we clambered up the mud to collect the gun. Like most puntguns she had an uncertain pedigree. The action was reputedly Greener's, the barrel from Holland's. Whatever, she patterned 20 oz of BBs beautifully at 60 yards.

With the big gun attached to her bows, the punt became a thing of killing beauty, sleek, shark-like. Broadside on, her 22 feet were all too obvious. But, end on, her kittiwake-grey decks sloping into the water, she practically vanished.

The ebb swept us down channel, past the marker buoys, past the shore gunners' saltings and into an estuarine world of mud, sands, winds,

126

water and wildfowl. We moored up. The mud, pock-marked with lugworm casts and holes, also bore the sinister scars of aircraft cannon. A spent round blended oddly with the cockle shells. This area was often used for target practice. Not today, though. The only airborne formations were those of brent geese cronking their way upwind, their call barely audible against the cracking of the ice.

It was February and it had been a hard winter. The flats were strewn with ice sheets, crazy-paving on a grand scale. Here and there the ice had compacted into ice-floes, glistening confections as high as four feet. Spectacular as they were, they would crush our punt in the narrow river's channel if we were too late returning on the tide.

We spied our ground. A blur of movement formed into a small party of wigeon skimming the sands. A bunch of mallard, six strong, bobbed 300 yards to our right. Nothing shootable. Slipping anchor, we cut down the starboard side of the channel, the tide pushing us past knots and dunlin dancing along the flow's edge.

'There. Do you see them?' My partner nodded towards twenty or so mallard drifting on the popple at a sandbank's edge. Punt-gunners have a sliding scale for fowl, the geese at the top, wigeon at the bottom. The more desirable the species, the fewer constitute a decent shot. Twenty mallard was well worth the powder.

'Right, we'll have a crack at them.' I pushed the cartridge into the breech and half-cocked the gun. Flattening myself onto the boards, I gathered the lanyard in my right hand, my face pressed into the salt-pickled wood, my legs crammed under the decking, the heavy weight of my partner pressing on the backs of my legs as, barely perceptibly, we set to the fowl.

The stalk is the prerogative of the experienced fowler. Using lead-tipped setting-poles and hand paddles, his is the sinew-straining task of sending the punt skimming towards the fowl. All the gunner has to do is align the gun with the thickest depth of wildfowl and judge, to a nicety, the moment to fire. A second too late – when the fowl have sprung – and his only reward will be his partner's wrath. The gunner sees little of the stalk, building a picture only with sound – the hiss of the bows, the sharp breathing of the 'setter', the soft whistling and growlings, the pipings and the quackings of the wildfowl. And the sound of his own heart.

This is a moment of unalloyed excitement, that same shiny joy experienced when you were a boy and the wigeon had chosen to flight over you that moment, a single cock falling to your panicked shot, its buffs, chestnuts and creams feather-perfect in the first light. Reality cannot tamper with this excitement since, face down, yours is a world only of sound, smell and motion.

'Have a look,' whispered my partner. I knew from his tone that the shot was off. Eighty yards off the mallard had paddled away from the sandbank to float in disconsolate clumps of twos and threes. Useless. Sitting up, we sent them quacking.

It was time to stretch the legs. We took a stroll over the sands and had lunch. The sun was now strong, hot, an odd contrast to the ice-floes surrounding us. Glinting eye-achingly white, a sandbank shimmered half a mile away, covered in ice. *Moving* ice?

'They can't be. They are!' It seemed that every pintail on the coast had gathered there, into an area no bigger than an acre and a half. Sandwiches forgotten, we clambered into the punt and headed for them. Heavy shots at pintail, that most elegant of duck, are rare. This day was no exception. What appeared a solid concourse of duck was actually made up of innumerable family groups of half a dozen, none of which was worth the shot. And we could not line up a collection of half-dozens since there were simply too many of them. Every time we closed, a group of heads would pop up, spot our broadside and raise the alarm. After ten minutes of this we withdrew, content just to watch the spectacle. No shot then, but the sight of that lump of pintail had been reward enough.

The sun and the sudden cessation of adrenalin induced torpor. Sprawled in the punt, we drank tea and waited for the tide to turn. My partner recounted how his friend sings to the seals, bringing them within feet of the boat, and of a time last year when they tailed a tope as it cruised past the punt. Except that it wasn't a tope; it was a small blue shark without a sense of humour.

Slack water – a time of suspension, of rest from the constant tidal struggle. We paddled round a spit and spied, half a mile away, a clump of about twenty-five wigeon on the edge of the sand. I pushed myself onto the deck, lanyard in hand. I sensed that we would have them and knew that my partner shared my feelings. Strange how fowling companions often attain a degree of telepathy, their minds attuned only to the hunting instinct. Five minutes passed. The steady swish of the water, the muted plop of the setting-poles. We were close now.

'Get ready.' His voice was hoarse with excitement. The shot was on. I eased myself up on my elbows and squinted down the gun. Twenty-two wigeon, nicely packed, were within 80 yards. They were all asleep, enjoying the sun's warmth. Completely wild birds, reared in the eastern wastes, they had survived migration and winter's harshness. But the fates dictated that they met us here, at this moment.

'Now,' he whispered. I pulled the lanyard and heard no sound, all senses obliterated by that of sight as through the smoke I watched a swathe being cut through the fowl and wigeon patter down like autumn leaves. My gaze was still transfixed as I ran across the sands, jamming a cartridge into the cripple-stopper. Two shots and the wingbeats ceased. We gathered the bag, a dozen in all. Not a heavy shot but a reasonable one in the circumstances.

We stashed the birds carefully under the decking and rigged the sail. The light was draining out of the sky. A dog barked from a Lincolnshire farmstead. The ice began chinking its way up river. Gurglings and bubblings, the song of the saltings, marked the tide's flow as it filled the shellfish blow-holes.

A single skein of pinks flighted high overhead as, wind in our sail, we made our way home.

CHAPTER XXXI

Chance of a Lifetime

JOHN RICHARDS

MY PUNTING partner Anthony had just returned from a week-long fowling trip in the north. On the evening he arrived home I telephoned, anxious first to learn of his exploits, and then to discuss two final days' punting before the end of the season. Winter had suddenly arrived with a vengeance and on our Welsh estuary hard frost and easterly winds had at last frozen the inner marsh. The pintail were coming to the low-water channel – it was the opportunity we had both been waiting for. An air of excitement prevailed as we discussed our rendezvous for 8.30 a.m. the next day.

On our river punting is as much a tradition as salmon netting, shrimping and cockling. The appearance of a vehicle towing the 24-foot gunning punt is nothing unusual. That morning Andy, a local fisherman, was checking his mooring and strolled across to help us launch the punt. He had been down the river the day before and said he had seen a stack of duck. Twenty minutes later we were aboard

130

the punt and slipping down the river past the old dock to where the grassy banks broaden out to the estuary.

As we rowed down the strong ebb an easterly wind eased our passage. When we were well down the river it was time to load the gun. I ran the punt ashore and Anthony wiped the surplus oil from the inside of the gun, tightened the breaching rope and attached the check chain. The gun was loaded and the breech screwed into place. Now that punt and gun were ready we carried on down the river until we reached the mast marking the navigation channel for the upper reaches. It offers an ideal vantage point which we climb to view the estuary, which stretches sixteen miles west and four miles to the north.

A mile and a half to the west I could see a small party of mallard; to the north there were pintail on the move. We were too early for the birds to settle as vast mudflats were only now appearing. Godwits, knots and redshanks followed the ebbing tide. Overhead a flock of golden plover, driven from the frozen pastures behind the sea-wall, called plaintively as they passed. We drank coffee as we waited and watched.

Through the glasses we could see the favourite pintail bank. It was five feet high and on the bend of the river three miles downstream. We knew that the birds did not normally come to the channel until low water and under the circumstances, with an easterly wind, a downwind stalk would be very unlikely to succeed. We decided to try to pass the mallard and push on downriver before the pintail came to the channel, in the hope that this would give us an upwind stalk with more cover from the riverbank. We set off again, leaving the river bank behind us. Before us the vast estuary stretched out as far as the eye could see.

Downstream we took stock of our position: the easterly wind had strengthened, we were on a thirty-foot spring tide and when the flood tide arrived the water would be very rough and no place for a shallow-draught gunning punt. Nevertheless, we had to wait as long as possible far down the estuary to allow the birds to come to their favourite roost.

We settled down for a long wait, watching the movement of the fowl in excited anticipation. It was now an hour after low water and we would see the flood tide in two hours' time. The first of the pintail had come from the back of the marsh to the narrow river channel three miles upstream. We lay low in the punt as more birds joined them.

Each party washed and preened and swam to the bank. Already two hundred birds were high and dry and as each minute passed more were joining them. It was time for us to make our move.

We had some way to go and at first we could both push against the wind and the ebbing tide. Nowadays it nearly always falls to me to push the punt but at that time we took it in turns. Anthony was the puntsman and I was the gunner. Under those conditions the puntsman had a tortuous job, almost levering the punt yard by yard through the water. He was spurred on by what now appeared to be an army of pintail arrayed like a football crowd on the terraces. Through the binoculars I could see the drakes' chocolate heads and the contrasting white necks and bellies. Even the immature drakes could be seen in contrast to the drab ducks. Here was clearly the chance of a lifetime.

We were now within 150 yards and the excitement mounted. Not a bird was aware of our presence and the bend of the river had hidden our silent approach. With a hundred yards to go I cocked the gun and my heart was beating audibly. We knew we had to make another thirty yards to get in range and it appeared that the birds were set back in a bay from the main channel.

As we made our final approach there was a faint rasp from the underside of the punt; we had touched a sandbank and in front of us now was only shallow water. The way was impassable. Our hearts fell. We were not in range and there was no hope of seeing the tide for at least an hour.

A moment later the nearest drakes' heads went up as they sensed danger. The birds rose as one into the wind and headed east up the estuary. We had been so close and yet so far from a really good shot.

The excitement had been intense but now our position was precarious. To stay where we were a moment longer would have meant we were stranded on the sandbank and we would then have to wait for the tide. Quickly we pulled the punt back to the deep water. Our only chance lay in the main channel a mile to the east. Sure enough, there were pintail on the bank, but not half the number we had previously seen. However, it would be a worthwhile shot if we could get to them.

I had changed with Anthony and was now pushing the punt. Yard by yard we approached the birds. We were now in range and I braced myself for the shot. The strangest thing suddenly happened. All the pintail started to run from the edge of the channel. Their heads were up and they were making a low nasal *kruck* alarm call. Seconds later the reason for their alarm became apparent. The tide was upon us, pushing all before it. Faced with the problems of picking birds on a spring tide, Anthony did not fire. In such circumstances it would have been dangerous to do anything else and the day was no less enjoyable for not having a shot.

It was time to head for home. The easterly wind was freshening and wind against tide soon made the water rough. We had a long row home but were already planning for the following day. It was to be equally exciting, but, in terms of duck, quite unrewarding. It was not until the following season that we finally made our shot at pintail and that is another story.

CHAPTER XXXII

The North Sea Surge

COLIN WILLOCK

THERE ARE those purists who put duck shooting and wildfowling in separate columns. Wildfowling, they say, is something that can only be done beyond the sea-wall. Duck shooting is an altogether tamer affair, practised on inland waters and, at the very lowest end of the scale, flight ponds. I dare say there is something in what they say but I have had some of my coldest, wettest, muddiest, most exciting and productive wildfowl shooting inland on the Ouse washes. But let that pass. This book is about wildfowling and for once I intend to satisfy the purists.

In those days, and I'm writing about the mid-1950s, we did all our wildfowling beyond the sea-wall, in the Medway estuary to be precise. At that time anyone could go anywhere on the foreshore. Only the most devoted went to Stoke Ooze. It is rightly named. The boot-clutching, body-plastering qualities of that mud exceeded anything produced in a glue factory. I don't know what renders that Medway ooze so oozy.

I have a feeling that it is partly because a great deal of the top layer of mud was removed in barges long ago by navvies engaged in puddling the beds of London reservoirs. Something like that, anyway. The result of these excavations is that dotted about the mudflats are islands which stand up rather like the mesas in Monument Valley, Arizona. Why the navvies didn't dig these out too, I have never understood. Possibly the earth wasn't of the right quality or was too hard even for them to work.

Anyway, there they stand, flat-topped, seldom more than fifty yards long, some a lot smaller. The plateau on top is covered with rough, salt-resistant grass. For some reason there is usually a wild rose bush or two growing there as well. How these get planted and take root, and why briers of all things should be favoured by the harsh marsh conditions, is another of Stoke's mysteries.

I owe my introduction to Stoke Ooze, and indeed to wildfowling, to the late Dick Arnold. Arnold got me into muzzle-loading. From that it was but a ramrod's shove to taking our muzzle-loaders down to the coast. But by the time of the expedition of which I am writing we had graduated, I recall, to breech-loaders, which shows that we were beginning to go soft.

The trouble about flighting at Stoke was that you could never get quite far enough out on a falling tide and always seemed to be retreating just ahead of a making one. In either case, the wigeon were always on the tide edge or just beyond it, so you were lucky if you ever really got amongst them. Later we were partially to solve this by means of a sneak-boat-cum-gun-punt, of which I have written in *The Gun-Punt Adventure*. Mention of this book introduces the third character in this story, Jack Hargreaves of television fame, with whom I then worked in Fleet Street. Jack it was who designed and built the punt, but I am getting ahead of events.

Just as Arnold had introduced me a few years before to wildfowling, so I now opened up this whole new world for Jack, a keen shooting man but one who had never shot a wigeon on the saltings. We planned his début with care. For a long time Dick Arnold and I had been scheming to plowter out over the muds to some of the more distant islands, maroon ourselves there while the tide built up round us, and stay out until the ebb left us high and, we hoped, dry. We picked a big tide so that every available duck would be flooded off and airborne. To take full advantage of the situation we had to leave the sea-wall at about 4.30 a.m. We would then reach our selected islands long before dawn broke. We told Jack that he was highly privileged to make his

135

first wildfowling expedition beyond the sea-wall in such experienced company and on such a momentous and well thought out expedition.

He did ask – very reasonably, I thought – whether we were quite sure that the islands selected remained above water at high tide. We laughed light-heartedly to allay his very proper apprehension. Privately it was something that had occurred to me, though possibly not to Arnold, a perpetual optimist. Come to think of it, I *had* seen a little flotsam or maybe jetsam, lying around on the grass on top of my island. I dismissed this as the product of a freak tide. It could never happen again.

We had, of course, consulted the tide tables. We had not, however, consulted the Met. Office. This, as it turned out, was a mistake.

Jack got his baptism by ooze almost as soon as he stepped into the first gutter in total darkness. Moving forward with considerable momentum, he left both his waders behind him in the mud and went in up to the hocks in his stockings. 'I never thought it would be like that' was all he said. On the whole he was very good about it.

I dropped Jack off on his island and then skated out over the muds a farther two hundred yards to mine. Dick Arnold was closer inshore but on a far smaller and rather lower island. The wind was now coming in off the North Sea at gale force. Lovely!

I settled down behind my rose bush, extending its cover with a short length of camouflage net. Almost as soon as the first crack of light appeared on the eastern horizon, a party of about ten teal came over my head so fast that I could only get a token shot off at them. I couldn't hear if the other two were shooting. You could barely hear your own gun in that shriek of wind. It wasn't supposed to be high tide until midday. Normally I wouldn't have expected to see any water making up the surrounding creeks until at least 10.30. By eight o'clock menacing brown bubbles were starting to course inshorewards over the shell bottoms of the gutters. It's the gale, I reassured myself – and so, to some extent, it was.

If I couldn't hear the other two shooting I could see Jack sending out his dog, and Dick floundering against the wind to retrieve birds that had fallen close by him on the mud. We were all, in the immortal phrase of the late Kenzie Thorpe, 'shooting pretty strong'. I am not sure that we were hitting equally 'strong'. The stuff was moving pretty fast on that howling gale. It was also swinging about quite a bit in the wind. One in five would be a fair estimate of kills to cartridges, maybe not even as good as that. When I wasn't shooting I was just watching open-mouthed.

THE NORTH SEA SURGE

We had been right about one thing. Everything *was* in the air. Every wader in the identification charts flew past; possibly some that weren't. I soon gave up blasting off at redshank and bar-tailed godwits. They were both on the statute book in those wicked days. A skein of greylags passed just out of shot. Wigeon were everywhere, though not all that often in range. Goldeneye rocketed past, as well as shovelers, the odd mallard, teal galore and pintail. I got a couple of drakes early on.

By 10 a.m. I'd picked ten wigeon, two pintail drakes and four teal. Even if it stopped there and then it would be a red-letter day for the notorious Stoke Ooze. And then, about 10.30, things began to get quieter. The wind hadn't dropped but it was less gusty, more purposeful and regular in its blowing, as if it was trying to push the whole North Sea in on top of us.

At eleven o'clock it began to occur to me that this might be what it actually *was* doing. The waters had risen to within six inches of the top of my island. I could see that Jack was in much the same situation, though his island had about six inches more freeboard than mine. As to Arnold, the top of the little dimple on which he was perched was already awash. And there was an hour to go to high water.

There were still odd parties of duck in the air, some of them passing within range. I didn't shoot at them any more. I didn't fancy risking the dog on the powerful tide that was now flowing. Anything hit fell a long way downwind and might be 150 yards away by the time the dog reached it. Instead I concentrated on keeping what I'd got, stringing the duck together so that they didn't float away. There was now a real danger of this happening. The water was well over the grass and still rising. I thought of all those old stories of wildfowlers standing on their dogs but Teal, my big old springer, didn't look as though he'd co-operate.

Midday came and the waters still rose. I could see that Arnold was over the top of his waders.I thought I saw him tying himself to his rose bush. All around was a waste of water. Not a single island remained above the surface. I broke a branch off my rose bush and hurled it out into the tide. I wasn't at all pleased to see that it continued voyaging quite rapidly towards the sea-wall. The tide was still making.

An hour and a half after the scheduled high tide, the water eased. I had an inch left before it poured down inside my thigh waders. Standing jammed up against my rose bush I had managed to keep myself from being blown over. It was hard to tell, but, at a quarter to two, I fancied there was half an inch more of my wader showing above the water level. At 2 p.m. an empty plastic bottle definitely halted its shoreward progress and started to head out to sea again.

It was well after dark when we finally met, soaked through, on the sea-wall. I was surprised to see Arnold at all. He affected not to have been worried. 'I got a little concerned', he admitted, 'when I saw a field mouse climbing my rose bush.'

Between us we had over thirty duck of six different species. Next day I phoned the Met. Office.

'You're very lucky,' the Met. Man said. 'Highest tide since the 1953 Canvey flood. You copped a North Sea surge. Why don't you ask us next time?'

Next time, I said, I most certainly would.

CHAPTER XXXIII

My Best Flight

ARTHUR CADMAN

IS THERE such a thing as a 'best flight'? To any wildfowler each successful flight could be the best. So I will start with my first flight, which was the best in many ways because it sowed the seeds of all my future wildfowling, seeds which fell on fertile ground.

It was near the River Windrush (more than fifty-five years ago) on a small pool in a swampy marsh. There were no duck on the pool when we arrived and as I knew nothing about duck flighting I wondered what we were doing there, when the pool was devoid of any wildfowl. On one side was a larch wood on a bank, on the other some tall poplars, all well away from us. Straight ahead was a glorious sunset.

Suddenly there was a quackering sound and seven shapes appeared out of that flaming sky. They circled, set their wings and came straight in. I remember no more. Indeed, it is immaterial whether or not a duck was shot – and is not that true of many a duck or goose flight? The magic of that lovely sight of those seven duck has held me in awe ever since, for I was intrigued with the eternal questions which every fowler must ask: 'Where have they come from? Why have they come here? Where will they go tomorrow?'

The very best flight? There have been so many: some because of the sights and sounds; some because of wonderful companions; many because of the bag, which is the least important, but more important if it is unexpected in regard to variety, or, just sometimes, numbers.

So I shall describe one evening which I shall remember for all time. My companion was a young wildfowler, twenty-one that very day. He had chosen to have a goose flight rather than a slap-up twenty-first birthday party in the local town. There was a terrific south-westerly gale as we went down to the marsh. I had Honey, then in her prime; my companion had Sam, one of Honey's offspring, which we had given him a couple of years before. Sam was developing into a good wildfowl dog.

We lined out about sixty yards apart and very soon a moderately good mallard and teal flight developed. Sam was pinching duck that I shot and when we had both shot half a dozen or so Honey could not put up with Sam's boisterous behaviour. She slipped away and brought them back to me from the little pile of duck behind my companion.

We were expecting geese – greys. But the light was almost gone before we heard the first geese. They came hedge-height and a little way to my right, so we moved. Then the most fantastic goose flight developed. Skein after skein of geese came, sweeping across the fields and over the marsh straight at us. We could just hear them above the sound of the gale and then they would be on top of us. The light was very bad and one could see even a great big greylag only when he was no more than twenty yards away.

Now a low goose, seen so close, presents an almost impossible shot. You cannot take him well out in front, because you can't see him then. You cannot shoot a goose ten or fifteen feet above your head – he is gone before the gun can be mounted, and to shoot him up the backside is not very rewarding. The first skein came over us without either of us getting our guns off at all.

'We need a butterfly net!' I shouted. 'Take the farthest from you, not the nearest.'

Indeed, that is the only way to deal with such a situation. The moment you see a goose in front, ignore him, and look down the line, picking a goose 25 or 30 yards away. I changed from heavy shot to No. 7s, and when the next skein came, a hundred or more, I took a goose out at the side and he plumped down into the rushes.

I do not know how many geese came over us that night. We were in the exact centre of an incredible flight, wave upon wave of greys, coming in huge numbers. Often there must have been 500 or more at one time, though we could only see the few in the centre. It was very rare to be able to get off both barrels because they were gone in a moment and there was only a split second to pick up a goose far enough away to shoot without smashing it.

Both dogs, mother and son, were working flat out. There was no question of stealing each other's geese. They had enough to do to find their own, for a goose that drops stone dead into dense rushes gives off little scent and often it is not so easy to find quickly. Under the circumstances, it was better to let the dogs pick up as quickly as possible, especially as the light was failing fast. We stopped shooting when we could not really see. But the geese were still coming, clamouring over us as very faint shapes. It had all lasted a comparatively short time, because the flight had started so late, but, even if the light had been still good enough to shoot, we would not have wished to shoot more.

Picking up took a little longer, but we did not lose a single goose, as we knew how many were down. We picked twelve fat greys and with the six or eight mallard and teal (I forget the exact number) that had been a fantastic flight for two guns. Of course, it was all the more memorable, because it was a twenty-first celebration, and because the two dogs, mother and son, worked so well and so happily. As the four of us trudged back to the car, laden with our spoils, there were no happier fowlers, or labradors, in the whole of the British Isles. The more so because it is Sod's Law that when there is an extra-special occasion, when one hopes for a splendid flight, things so often 'gang agley'.

I must mention one other momentous flight on one of the best goose lochs in all Europe. It was a flat calm evening, hopeless by any standards. Bear, my wonderful goose dog, and Honey, then a young girl, and I were sitting in a sunken pit beside the loch and the whole of the western sky was flaming red. Out of the sky came skein after skein of pinks and the whole loch rang with their calling, as each skein, some nearly a thousand strong, set their wings and planed down into the centre of the loch. Soon there was a great dark mass of geese on the water half a mile away.

Suddenly there was a huge commotion. Perhaps a mink had taken a goose in their midst. With a deafening clamour they rose and flew low across the water, straight for me and settled. I estimated that I had 2,000 pinks on the water within thirty yards, some of course much closer, and many more farther out. What a sight! What a sound!

As the last light faded, so their calling became a gentle murmur and, at last, silence. I sat there in wonder. If I had ever enjoyed one of nature's finest spectacles more, I do not remember it. I had to wait until it was almost pitch-dark (actually it never is as black as that) before I and my two dogs could creep away, without one goose knowing that a man with a 3-inch magnum had been so close to them.

Perhaps, after all, that was the very best flight. But there have been so many outstanding flights in a lifetime of fowling. For years it was my ambition to shoot a wiffling goose. When that happened – an 8 lb greylag, wiffling from a great height – it was a special occasion. How fast was he going? Your guess is as good as mine – maybe 70 miles per hour. His wings folded and he plunged with a loud *thwock* deep into the marsh.

Read's Island, on Humber, and wigeon coming in waves after the spring tide had flooded the frozen saltings. For once I shot far above my average, taking a right-and-left and a quick reload out of several packs. They were falling faster than my dog, a very speedy labrador, could bring them back, but he did not lose one. What a flight that was!

Tregaron Bog – the morning when the Greenland whitefronts decided to come to a tiny rushy pool. Two of us shot seven in as many minutes crouching in the rushes, and then it was all over. That was on a shoot where two geese in a month was about usual. The seven included the wing-tipped gander which became the forefather of all the early Greenlands to be bred in Britain.

The truth is that to a keen wildfowler almost every flight is the best, and not only the successful ones. The only flight that is not good is when you see naught and hear naught – and fill both your thigh boots.

CHAPTER XXXIV

Pinkfeet and Blue Toes

DAVID CAMPBELL

WITH RELIEF, we eventually came to a halt alongside the merse (or marsh as it's known on the English side of the Solway) after our long haul from home on the Scottish side. Twice we had come close to aborting our expedition as savage snowstorms blew up and blotted out the moon. Once we even turned the car round and headed back home. Thankfully, again the storm passed and our mission was on once more.

An icy blast cut into us as we stepped from the car, but the snow showers had passed and the sky was perfect for flighting. This was the first time Allan and I had ventured onto this merse. Word had filtered through from Carlisle that pinkfeet were moving under the moon and shooting chances were good.

Hurriedly we pulled on our waders and Barbours, both of us impatient to be on the merse. We could hear the geese out on the sandbanks beginning to stir as the tide began to invade their roost. It wouldn't be long before they would flight.

Cursing our stupidity for not walking over the merse during daylight hours, we stumbled along looking for a suitable creek or hole to hide in. Luck would have to be our main ally tonight for the flightlines on this merse were unknown to us all.

Even with the exertions of our 'yomp' over this unknown merse, the intense cold was already taking a grip and we were thankful for our thermal long johns and extra pullover, but our ears, nose and feet had begun to tingle.

The geese had become very active, floating in towards the bank before lifting and moving farther out again. Finding an ambush place was now urgent. We decided to drop into the next ditch we came upon. Allan positioned himself at the mouth of the creek while I moved about 30 yards along. Laying down my groundsheet, I went through the usual ritual of battling with Toby, my labrador, for an equal share. Honours shared, we settled down.

An hour later we still crouched there, desperately trying to fight off the cold, though Toby warmed me a little. Geese were flighting all the time now but as yet none had come anywhere near us. Thoughts of calling it a night were beginning to occupy my mind when suddenly Allan's shout of 'Geese' brought me to attention.

A glance over the top revealed a skein of about twenty bearing down on us. I growled at Toby to sit still and flattened myself against the bank. On they came, in fine voice. My grip on the 10-bore tightened as the adrenalin started to flow. Although I have been in the same position many times since my early teens, the thrill and excitement of it all remain the same.

As the geese crossed the floodbank I heard Allan's two shots ring out, followed by a heavy thump which didn't seem too far from me, and then I stood up and pulled through the bird of my choice. My first shot missed. Trying not to panic, I carried on through and fired again. This time there was no mistake. He threw his head back and fell dead twenty yards behind me. Toby soon had him to hand.

Allan came over to pick up his goose, which was lying on its back a few feet in front of me, and explained he'd sent Gun, his labrador, off to look for a second bird that he was certain he'd seen plane out. And a few minutes later Gun arrived back with a pink, which was dispatched quickly and efficiently by Allan before we slipped another couple of shells in the gun and moved back to our positions.

Suddenly I felt quite warm and we had the enthusiasm to hang on another half-hour or so. An hour later, with the cold again penetrating our defences and the tide starting to creep up our waders, we decided to call it a night, disappointed that nothing else had come close enough for a shot.

What greeted us when we climbed from our ditches gave us one of the biggest frights we have had since we started fowling and emphasized the folly of going on a strange merse, especially in the moonlight, without daylight reconnaissance. The tide had run up and overflowed most of the ditches and creeks around us and for a split second we thought we had been cut off. However, after taking stock of the situation we decided that if we made our way up the merse, away from where the car was parked, we should manage to get off.

Without wasting any more time we picked our birds up and made off in all haste.

We had walked barely 100 yards when a stroke of luck befell us. A skein of pinks came straight towards us. I fumbled a couple of shells into the 10-bore and dropped to my knees. Allan did the same.

On they came, seemingly oblivious to us. I stood up and fired as they crossed our position. I heard my first shot strike home and saw my bird set its wings and plane down into the tide behind us. My second shot missed handsomely. Allan had failed to score with both shots – unusual for him. Toby retrieved as we made our way to dry land.

We arrived back at the car very weary and cold and the dogs were briskly rubbed down before we set off home with the heater going full blast.

However, even the journey home was not without incident. As we rounded a bend we were faced with a huge expanse of water which completely covered the road. A half-submerged sign read 'When the water reaches this point it is two feet deep', which put paid to any attempt to ford it. There was nothing else we could do but turn back and make a long detour through Anthorn village, which was also flooded, but, with me walking in front to give Allan an indication of depth, we managed to get through.

It was 3.30 a.m. as I crept into the house, trying hard not to waken my family. The moon still glistened on the ebbing tide as I looked out of the window. Geese would be on the move all night and render a morning flight useless. I could have a lie-in and start to plan another flight for tomorrow.

CHAPTER XXXV

A Quartet of Pinks

PETER WHITAKER

THE DYKE drives straight and true as a broadsword deep into the blackheart of the fen, severing subterranean veins that seep into this peat-stained artery. At the foot of the sea-bank on the landward side, where the Delph crosses it to form its hilt, the waters build against a sluice through which the pumping station at the pommel hurries the overspill seawards after winter rains.

The outfall creek that winds towards the tideline among the saltings is a deep and treacherous channel even at low water. A few narrow plank bridges, familiar only to wildfowlers and bait diggers, permit precarious passage to the endless mudflats which stretch like a shimmering moonscape to the edge of the distant tide. Where the saltings end and sea lavender and crab-grass give way to patches of weed and trailing fronds of eel-grass among shallow pans where sandy tide ripples, like knuckle marks in soft putty, are the only relief in a monotony of mud, the channel snakes into an S-bend. There a million ebbing spring tides under as many moons have undercut the bank

146

into a steep overhang below which the silt, swept downstream into the eddy, has built up into a tiny beach which forms a firm but narrow foothold on the edge of the slimy ooze. This is a good place to be at dawn when the tide is still running out, the wind is a point or two west of south and the geese are roosting on the high sands a mile or more out to sea.

That is where we had been yesterday, spread out between this snug little indentation and the lower bulge of the S-bend, having watched the skeins flight out directly over this spot on the previous evening. But, although by dawn the wind's strength and direction seemed not to have changed, the flight line had. Perhaps unexpected boat traffic in the shipping lane had disturbed the geese, the main body of which came in lower down the coast. On the extreme left of our line only a single small skein offered a chance, which was squandered by the excited, premature discharge of the only 8-bore in the party.

This morning, with my companions recalled to their desks, I was on my own. Except for an overnight frost, weather conditions remained unchanged, so it seemed sensible to return to the same ambush. Even if most of the geese flighted wide, I reasoned, that was where most of the competition would be and one's chance of success is often greater with small parties than against the main concentration. Thus the fact that only one other fowler appeared to have chosen the same stretch of foreshore in no way disappointed me. As we made ready I noticed a number of silhouette goose decoys in the boot of his car and wondered what use he might have for them this morning. It transpired that they were simply part of his stock-in-trade, employed on the foreshore only very early in the season before new arrivals of young geese become wise to their false impression. We discussed decoys for a moment, in particular the American mega-goose model in foam and fibreglass. Eight feet long it is claimed to attract Canada geese from three miles away. Whatever the truth of this, we concluded that it might usefully serve as a liferaft.

Going my separate way, I was pleased to see no footprints of earlier risers in the glistening rime on the bridges. Under a few late stars I followed the familiar landmarks to the mud and turned left along the edge of the big gutter. Stopping now and again to listen out, I heard no murmur of goose talk from the direction of the sea, but the spring tide was a long way out and so too would be any geese.

The time of decision came when I arrived at the bank's overhang above the patch of hard standing. Should I settle here or move on a little farther to the place where the geese had crossed yesterday? I tried to take a goose's-eye view. This bend on the corner of the main gutter looked to me very much like a local landmark on a flight path; but, with the previous experience fresh in mind, I made the second choice.

I had hardly settled into position with the dog tucked tight against the creekside when I sensed something watching me. Looking over my shoulder, I saw a seal staring at us from the middle of the fast-ebbing stream in the emptying gutter. There it remained, eyes fixed on my back, until ridiculously I began to feel uncomfortable. Finally I dug deep beneath my fowling coat for a penny piece which I threw at the sleek, dark-grey head to make it go away. The gesture was futile: the seal remained *in situ* and was still watching when three pinkfeet coming straight off the sea followed the mud to fly at head height directly over the position I had rejected earlier. Helplessly I watched them fly inland well clear of the other gunner back on the saltings and turned back to my audience. But the seal had gone, no doubt laughing all the way to the sandbanks.

Disappointed, I had just climbed up onto the open mud when a faint double call from the right caught my ear. Instinctively I fell flat on my face in a convenient shallow depression, pinning the dog beneath me. Accustomed to such antics, he showed no surprise, but his tail thumped under my left arm as he sensed approaching geese and I followed his gaze half right of where we lay. There, approaching swiftly and almost silently, with pinions almost brushing the mud, were four geese. As they swept past behind us only a few yards away, I somehow managed to raise myself to my haunches, swivel round and awkwardly, against the natural swing of the body, fire both barrels at the two nearest birds.

The first shot winged a goose, which fell on the far side of the big gutter to be retrieved by the dog before it got to the water. The second apparently had no effect. As soon as it was full daylight and clear that no more geese would come, we made our way back across the saltings to where I had left the car.

There waiting for us was the other wildfowler holding a pinkfooted goose.

'Yours, I think,' he said before I could congratulate him. Mortally struck by my second shot, it had fallen fifty yards from him as he waited in vain on the flank a long way behind me.

That's what I call a gentleman gunner. It was the last day of the season and my first right-and-left at geese on the foreshore.